T0306085

AI and Education in China

This book explores the relationships between artificial intelligence (AI) and education in China. It examines educational activity in the context of profound technological interventions, far-reaching national policy, and multifaceted cultural settings. By standing at the intersection of three foundational topics – AI and the recent proliferation of data-driven technologies; education, the most foundational of our social institutions in terms of actively shaping societies and individuals; and, finally, China, which is a frequent subject for dramatic media reports about both technology and education – this book offers an insightful view of the contexts that underpin the use of AI in education, and promotes a more in-depth understanding of China.

Scholars of educational technology and digital education will find this book an indispensable guide to the ways new technologies are imagined to transform the future, while being firmly grounded in the past.

Jeremy Knox is Senior Lecturer at the University of Edinburgh and Co-director of the Centre for Research in Digital Education. His research interests include the relationships between education, data-driven technologies, and wider society, and he has led projects funded by the Economic and Social Research Council (ESRC) and the British Council in the UK. Jeremy's published work includes *Posthumanism and the MOOC: contaminating the subject of global education* in 2016.

AI and Education in China

Imagining the Future, Excavating the Past

Jeremy Knox

Routledge
Taylor & Francis Group

LONDON AND NEW YORK

First published 2023
by Routledge
4 Park Square, Milton Park, Abingdon, Oxon OX14 4RN

and by Routledge
605 Third Avenue, New York, NY 10158

Routledge is an imprint of the Taylor & Francis Group, an informa business

© 2023 Jeremy Knox

British Library Cataloguing in Publication Data
A catalogue record for this book is available from the British Library

ISBN: 978-1-032-44951-7 (hbk)
ISBN: 978-1-032-45044-5 (pbk)
ISBN: 978-1-003-37513-5 (ebk)

DOI: 10.4324/9781003375135

Typeset in Times New Roman
by codeMantra

To Humphrey, and your future

Contents

Acknowledgements

There are many colleagues whose interest, collaboration, constructive criticism, and corridor conversations have directly and indirectly influenced this book. In particular, I would like to thank colleagues at the Centre for Research in Digital Education at the University of Edinburgh for providing the supportive and fertile research environment in which this book was conceived. Dr Li Yuan and Dr Tore Hoel have also provided many ideas, insights, and provocations that have greatly shaped my understanding through our collaborative research of Artificial Intelligence in Education and China. Dr Wei Cui has been an additionally generous and insightful collaborator.

I would also like to thank Dr Ben Williamson and Dr Rebecca Eynon as editors of a special issue of Learning Media and Technology entitled *AI and Education: critical perspectives and alternative futures*, in which I was able to publish some of the initial ideas that eventually formed into this book.

Finally, I would like to thank Yuchen for the immense support with writing this book, the incomparable advice and guidance about the challenging subjects I have tried to elucidate, and the unfathomable supply of encouragement and inspiration that has kept me going. This book is thoroughly indebted to your generosity, wisdom, and strength.

1   Introduction

This book is about the relationships between artificial intelligence (AI) and education in China. It is primarily a book about education, which centres educational concerns, and aims to address a readership interested in this particular area of research and practice. However, it is also a book that, as will be argued in this introduction, necessarily functions across and engages a number of disciplines, attempting as it does to examine education in the context of profound technological interventions, far-reaching national policy, and multifaceted cultural settings. As such, this book is about the intersection of three foundational topics: first, *AI* and the recent proliferation of data-driven technologies which are increasingly assumed to usher in profound transformations in society, from grand prognostications of economic revolutions to the everyday experiences of algorithmically infused decision-making; second, *education*, perhaps the most foundational of our social institutions in terms of actively shaping societies and individuals, and one that is increasingly targeted for technological disruptions; and, finally, *China*, which itself appears to be a frequent subject for dramatic media reports about both technology and education, being perceived equally as an ascendant world (AI) power and a deeply traditional (educational) culture. What this book offers, therefore, is an in-depth examination of the junctures between these topics, in ways that excavate fresh and critical insights about the growth of AI internationally, its foundational and interdependent relationship with the education sector, set against the backdrop of a country whose radical economic and technological rise seems to be matched only by an increasing fascination from the rest of the world.

While this book also sets out to appeal to readers interested in each of these foci – AI, education, and China – it does so with an explicit emphasis on interdisciplinary correspondences and overarching themes. The particular intersection of these themes, it is argued here, is vitally important for enriching the understanding of each topic individually. In other words, in order to grasp the current fixation on AI technologies, we need to apprehend, not only the education systems that are being re-envisioned to drive a perceived future of datafication and automation, but also the Chinese policies and private sector entrepreneurialism which are propelling the idea of

DOI: 10.4324/9781003375135-1

an AI-infused society. Additionally, in order to understand the trajectory of the project of education itself, broadly conceived, we need to examine, not only the ways in which AI technologies are envisioned as powerful actors, able to shape educational governance and learner subjectivity, but also the national contexts in which these developments appear to be accelerating most explicitly. Furthermore, in order to comprehend China at this particular time, we need to engage, not only with the ways AI technologies are being amalgamated into a broader vision of Chinese nationhood, citizenship, and culture, but also with the foundational role of education as a core institution involved in the formation of its society. Examining these relationships between AI and education in China, therefore, provides a rich and pertinent context for understanding the development of data-driven technologies internationally, and the broader understanding and practice of education in our times.

As a way of working through this particular intersection, and across the foci of AI, education, and China, the various chapters of this book will foreground both future imaginaries that seek to define the ways technological changes come about, and the underlying historical contexts that lie beneath the surface of more recent accounts of technical development and educational success. Indeed, a key focus of this book is to delve beyond uncritical readings of straightforwardly innovative AI, narrow renditions of 'enhanced' educational practices, and familiar characterisations of China, in order to trace the ways in which the future is being envisioned, and excavate the circumstances through which these very ideas have become possible to imagine. Two central perspectives that have informed the analytical approach in this book are therefore: sociotechnical imaginaries, offering methods that can examine future visions of technology and account for the ways they shape social order; and political and social history, which can reveal important precedents for contemporary phenomena, suggest underlying contexts through which specific visions of the future can be better understood, and reveal hidden histories often erased by the discourses and imaginings of AI. The following sections will outline these conceptual influences as a way of clarifying the analytical approach adopted in the subsequent chapters.

Sociotechnical imaginaries of AI

Jasanoff and Kim (2015) define a 'sociotechnical imaginary' thusly:

> collectively held, institutionally stabilized, and publicly performed vision of desirable futures, animated by shared understandings of forms of social life and social order attainable through, and supportive of, advances in science and technology.
>
> (Jasanoff and Kim 2015, p4)

In this way, they call attention to the ways visions of the future have substantial analytical value, for the ways they reveal societal norms in the present, and uncover the structures of power through which technologies, societies, and futures, are made. Sociotechnical imaginaries thus build upon a rich tradition of scholarship that has sought to trace the intimate and co-constitutive relations between technologies and society, as opposed to more dominant discourses of determinism and solutionism (e.g. Morozov 2013; Hamilton and Friesen 2013) that tend to portray technology as separate domain of pure scientific engineering. Technologies are thus considered to be in 'constant interplay with the social arrangements that inspire and sustain their production' (Jasanoff 2015a, p2). This perspective is particularly important for the field of education research, with has long maintained an artificial disjunction between 'human' learning and 'technical' enhancement (Bayne 2015). Further, sociotechnical imaginaries are employed in research to 'understand the co-production of technoscientific projects, social constellations, and politics' (Mager and Katzenbach 2021, p225), and it is this orientation that will support an in-depth study of the relationships between government strategy, AI development, and education practice.

Sociotechnical imaginaries are thus important ways of examining how the development of science and technology is situated within broader political and institutional practices, and it is from such a perspective that the coming into being of technologies can be linked to notions of structural power. Examining visions of the future offered by both state and private sector actors therefore offers a key way of tracing the production of sociotechnical imaginaries, and the ways they intermingle, coalesce, and compete in the materialisations of specific technologies and social orderings. As Mager and Katzenbach suggest, while technology companies 'dig into the rich pool of cultural norms, visions, and values to support digital tools and artifacts', and thus market them as solutions to pressing social problems, 'policy and public institutions promote their roadmaps, rules, and regulations' (2021, p224). It is through these powerful combinations of future imaginaries that the relationships between AI and education in China will be examined across the subsequent chapters of this book.

Crucially, sociotechnical imaginaries should be understood, not simply as imagination, illusion, or conjecture, but rather as powerful discourse that concretely shapes the ways technologies and societies form. Sociotechnical imaginaries 'solidify and institutionalise' (Mager and Katzenbach 2021, p228), rather than simply imagine:

> By guiding the making of things and services to come, imaginations of the future are co-producing the very future they envision. Hence, future visions are performative.
>
> (Mager and Katzenbach 2021, p224)

This performativity means that sociotechnical imaginaries can be viewed as crucially important indications, not only of the ways the future might unfold, but also of the prominent actors and voices who appear to be defining the vision. Importantly, it is in this performative dimension that sociotechnical imaginaries are often distinguished in a formal sense from other concepts, such as 'visions', 'notions', 'narratives', or simply 'discourse' about the future (Mager and Katzenbach 2021). This book adopts a looser approach to these terms, often using them interchangeably to explore, in general, a 'coming into being of AI as a key sociotechnical institution of the 21st century' (Bareis and Katzenbach 2022, p857). This less formal use is partially for stylistic reasons, but it is also an attempt to avoid the inference of definitive, bounded, and 'grand' sociotechnical imaginaries, as opposed to messier, overlapping, and divergent ideas about the future of AI.

This book takes forward the notion that analysing sociotechnical imaginaries offers three principal insights. First, *values*. Whenever the future of technology is imagined, whether involving hopes and desires for a better world, or fears and anxieties about deterioration and decline, it reveals important insights about the values that underpin the vision. For example, where AI is hailed as delivering new kinds of affordable personalisation in the classroom, or condemned as threatening to replace teachers, both visions comprise rich assumptions that expose social values, related to both education and technology. Here, one might infer a valuing of the idea of individualised, one-to-one teaching, as well as a regard for teaching labour. That these values are oppositional (automation being linked to the disruption of labour), yet coexist, is also important, demonstrating the ways that imaginaries are multiple, overlapping, contested, and often conflicting (Mager and Katzenbach 2021). The extent to which one imaginary of AI teaching might become dominant over the other, for example, the valorisation of personalised learning platforms over the protection of the teaching profession, relates to the second insight: *power*. Examining sociotechnical imaginaries offers the possibility of uncovering the ways particular visions of the future become dominant, and which actors are involved in propagating them. This is an important way of understanding future visions as often grounded within specific discourses, and emanating from particular communities and affiliations. Imaginaries, of course, also proliferate, combine, and overlap, across different actors, and in this sense are not necessarily traceable to defined origins. For example, as will be examined further in Chapters 3 and 7, the vision of AI-driven platforms providing personalised learning to diverse populations of students has become a powerful sociotechnical imaginary in China (and also elsewhere), due to a range of coalescing discourses, from policy-makers, entrepreneurial technology developers, 'ed tech' companies, regional education authorities, and (some) teachers. As such, imaginaries of AI's efficiency, precision, and objectivity in education tend to overshadow and obscure the voices of students, teachers, and other educators who might propose conflicting accounts. Both the identification of power and the exposing of values relate to the third insight, *performativity*. Examining sociotechnical imaginaries offers ways of understanding how technologies are guided into being, 'concretely constructed, made, and unmade in different constellations and contexts' (Mager and Katzenbach 2021, p224). In this way, imaginaries are not simply falsehoods that need disproving, but rather visions of the future that have a social function, and that contribute to the very real production, understanding, and governance of AI technologies. By projecting into the future, sociotechnical imaginaries end up establishing convincing sets of ideas about technology that play a substantial role in shaping and influencing how those technologies are made. Understanding imaginaries, therefore, offers crucial insight into the contingent processes through which AI technologies form, culturally, politically, socially, and technically.

It is important therefore to underscore that the imaginaries of AI suggested across this book are neither monolithic nor driven by a single governing actor. Rather, as the subsequent chapters will demonstrate, there are multiple contested visions of AI, which sometimes clash, intersect, or complement one another. The underlying tension is between, on the one hand, the regulatory practices of the state, which tend to perceive AI as a means to develop the economy, but also to manage and shape education towards the efficient production of human capital, and, on the other hand, the commercial and entrepreneurial activities of the private sector, which valorise innovation, and are focused on the generation of new (educational) markets for AI. There are also other competing and overlapping visions that will be brought to the fore across the subsequent chapters, underscoring the view that sociotechnical imaginaries are multiple, contested, and commodified (Mager and Katzenbach 2021). The point of this book, of course, is not to establish a singular explanatory sociotechnical imaginary, but rather to surface and examine the many visions of AI and education in China that often overlap, contrast, compete, and interlink with one another. The following chapters, on the themes of policy, the private sector, regulation, regional differences, expertise, and personalisation, all suggest different kinds of sociotechnical imaginaries that in their combination offer a general picture of the ways AI and education are being anticipated, designed, and governed in China. However, it is a combination that is loosely held together, precarious, and with many shifting parts, and the purpose of this book is certainly not to predict the future with any certainty. Rather, the focus on sociotechnical imaginaries is precisely to foreground contingency, and to trace the ways visions are contested and contestable. Imaginaries themselves are fragile, untrustworthy, and often incoherent. While each chapter (apart from Chapter 4) begins with articulating a particular future vision related to AI and education, its examination and analysis is intended to expose its instability, and indeed its often-multiple internal contradictions. This inclination to deconstruct the simplistic visions of AI-driven futures leads to the second conceptual focus that underpins this book.

Political and social history in China

As Brown contends, understanding China is nothing less than 'impossible' without at least some engagement with history, an orientation that becomes particularly vital where 'Chinese histories are not well known by people in Europe or the United States' (2020, p1). This book therefore seeks to illuminate key aspects of China's recent political and social history, as a way of establishing the contexts through which the current fascination with AI has derived. The aim here is to situate the various sociotechnical imaginaries of AI emerging from China, not exclusively amongst a general set of assumptions about the capacity of the technology, but rather within historical events, societal shifts, and educational reforms that are specific to China. This does not mean that sociotechnical imaginaries emerging from China are assumed to be entirely distinctive, and it is certainly the case, as will be revealed across the subsequent chapters, that more general assumptions about AI's instrumental role in societal and economic transformations are mirrored in much of Chinese discourse. However, historical insights, it is argued, offer additional dimensions that modulate and inflect the visions of AI-driven futures with often long-standing political currents and social patters. In such a way, political and social history is drawn upon in this book to deepen the understanding of sociotechnical imaginaries of AI, by grounding future projections of technology-infused education in the contexts that have made them possible. In other words, only by examining China's history can a richer understanding be developed of how and why particular visions of the future have formed, coalesced, and become dominant in the unfolding relationships between AI and education.

While it is, of course, beyond the scope of this book to provide a detailed account of China's recent history, a brief outline of some of the key political events of the previous century provide crucial insight for the understanding of the current focus on AI. Drawing on political (Brown 2020) and social (Kleinman et al. 2011) history, the subsequent chapters will principally focus on three periods: the reformism that ushered in the Republic of China until 1949; Maoist socialism and the establishment of the People's Republic of China (PRC); and, perhaps most importantly, the market reforms beginning in the late 1970s. Central to the discussion of these periods will be Lin's triad of 'nationalism, socialism, and developmentalism' (2006, p15), developed to analyse the period of China's socialist modernisation after 1949. This framework will be used to ground various themes across the book, and offer a way of understanding the dynamics of Chinese governance across the 20th century and into the present. For Lin, these three elements operate in close relation as the underlying ideological justifications of the Chinese state: '[n]ationalism denotes national unity, sovereignty, and autonomy; socialism stands for equality and social justice; and developmentalism implies a determination to overcome backwardness' (Lin 2006, p60). However, far from constituting any kind of natural balance or order, the ideals of nationalism, socialism, and developmentalism have formed a shifting set of tensions, through which differing visions of the Chinese state have been legitimised and contested. Lin explains the triadic relationship thusly:

> Together, national pride, socialist ambition, and economic drive underlay the Chinese desire for distinction and international recognition. Because of their intrinsic interconnection, the potential conflicts among these three dimensions can be reconciled in principle and can be dealt with through strategic adjustment insofar as China remains defiant to capitalist subordination. These forces are tied to each other but also are in competition, and as such inform policy negotiations and decisions. Their meanings and structural equilibrium, however, have not been fixed but rather are constantly contested in varying domestic and external conditions over the past more than half a century since 1949.
>
> (Lin 2006, p60)

In other words, nationalism, socialism, and developmentalism have not always been equally prominent in the functioning of the Chinese state, and an analysis of which elements have been emphasised, or indeed tempered, at any given time offers valuable insight into the ways governance is both maintained and modified for particular historical contexts. Indeed, while such a framework may be especially useful for understanding the emergence of the Chinese state after 1949, its value endures as an insight into the persistence of the ideological foundations of government. For example, where China is often described as straddling 'socialist legacies and a global capitalist economy' (Guo 2021, p3), the triadic relationship offers some understanding of the ways such an apparent tension is held together through, in one sense, the aligning of a market-driven economy with developmentalism and the improvement of public welfare, and further as a matter of strengthening the economic autonomy of the nation under the stewardship of a socialist government. Thus, the triadic framework offers a way to overcome simplistic accounts of the supposed opposition between capitalism and socialism in China, as well as suggest more nuanced ways in which differing ideologies compete (of course, in the above example, a global capitalist economy can be seen to undermine the ideals of social justice and equality, while at the same time challenging the relevance of the nation state). For the purposes of this book, the triad provides a worthwhile opportunity to consider the ways in which particular educational and technological developments might (mis)align with state ideology, and thus the broader contexts through which the imaginaries of AI innovation and education reform are made possible.

Alongside examining the ways Chinese governance can inform contemporary discussions of technology, surfacing political and social history itself is a vital aspect of developing critical understanding, precisely because much of the promotional discourse around AI obscures the past in order to valorise the future. As Mosco suggests in a discussion of the value of myths, akin to the scope of sociotechnical imaginaries:

> The denial of history is central to understanding myth as depoliticized speech because to deny history is to remove from discussion active human agency, the constraints of social structure, and the real world of politics.
>
> (Mosco 2005, p35)

In just this way, the inclusion of political and social history in this book is intended to repoliticise the discourses around AI, specifically in ways that emphasise human decision-making, contingency, and power. Directly in relation to the discourses around AI, Vallor questions a similar denial of history:

> to think of AI only in the context of what is new and ahead, is also serving a political purpose, and a very regressive one. History teaches us of patterns and dynamics that are still acting on us today, and that continue to shape choices being made about the use of new technologies.
>
> (Vallor 2021)

This underscores the critical value of the historical insights examined throughout this book, which not only act as a counter to the ahistorical imaginaries of AI futures in China, but also surface undercurrents and resonances from the past that actively contribute to the making of the future. Furthermore, attempting to associate and juxtapose future projections of AI with China's history serves to critically ground the celebratory discourses of technology-driven futures, and acknowledge the underlying political and social contexts through which such technologies are produced and deployed. In this sense, the inclusion of political and social history is influenced by the method of genealogical analysis, concerned with the ways 'contemporary practices and institutions emerged out of specific struggles, conflicts, alliances, and exercises of power' (Garland 2014, p372). For Ball, this approach is 'a way of demonstrating uncertainty and contingency' (2013, p33), which is particularly important to uncover as a counter to the more mainstream discourses of inevitable technological progress, which tends to pervade the imaginaries of AI. A central underlying critical thread running through this book is therefore an intention to expose: the ways AI technologies have come to be imagined as 'innovative' and 'revolutionary'; the conditions through which education has been made both amenable to AI interventions and a necessary foundation for their advancement; and, crucially, the contexts that shape outsider perspectives on, and assumptions about, Chinese politics, society, and culture. As Ball further contends, '[w]hat seems "natural" or truthful or inevitable is in fact enabled by clashes of forces, everything has a history and has lowly beginnings.' (2013, p34). The conditions for examining such foundations are necessarily wide-ranging, involving, not only historical contexts, but also the current policy landscape in China, its burgeoning entrepreneurial technology sector, its cities and regions, and its diaspora, as well as the ways individuals and society have been conceptualised over time. Through these broad themes, this book seeks to 'problematize the present by revealing the power relations upon which it depends and the contingent processes that have brought it into being' (Garland 2014, 372), and to focus this critical lens specifically on the proliferating discourses and imaginaries of AI innovation and educational reform.

Importantly, accompanying the analysis of sociotechnical imaginaries with historical insight, as is the structure of most of the chapters, is not devised to suggest any kind of grand narrative about the Chinese context. Rather, the historical insights in this book are offered as ways of acknowledging that sociotechnical imaginaries, despite often being focused around novel technologies and practices, as is the case with AI, are grounded in sometimes long-held ideas and assumptions, social patterns, and political dynamics. Historical contexts, therefore, do not necessarily nor straightforwardly explain or justify a particular vision of the future, but the connection helps to acknowledge that imaginaries do not simply spring untethered from the present. Rather, particular imaginaries only become possible because of the way historical contexts shape the present. Of course, this also makes history a matter of interpretation, and the contexts drawn upon in this book are certainly not proposed as definitive or incontestable accounts of past events, only readings which serve the purpose of grounding sociotechnical imaginaries in exploratory and analytically useful ways. This is particularly important to emphasise in the context of writing about China, which is so often portrayed in grand, monolithic terms (Chu 2013). As Lin further suggests, China should be understood, not as a static entity within an appointed global order, but rather in terms of 'vast internal diversity and diverse external influences' (Lin 2013, p3). As such, 'neither the Chinese state nor Chinese society can ever be treated as a coherent monolith – there is never anything like a singular, authentic "Chineseness" to speak of' (Lin 2013, p3). Following Lin, therefore, the use of political and social history in this book sets out to avoid positioning China as a mere 'given', rather acknowledging that there are always the questions of 'which China', and 'who speaks for it and why' (2013, p4).

While the foreground of this book is an examination of the relationships between AI and education, the background and specific setting for this investigation is China, its governance, economy, and geography, but also its society and culture. In this sense, this book is also a study of China; however, it is necessarily a highly selective one, in which the country is seen specifically through a limited set of historical events and periods, and through the lens of particular educational policies. Nevertheless, due to the prominence of AI in current strategic visions for the country, such perspectives offer important insights for the study of China itself. As such, this book is generally oriented towards how the rest of the world might view China, as opposed to how the Chinese might view themselves. In other words, while the ultimate aim is to generate a wider understanding of the Chinese context, the subsequent chapters are often quite overtly concerned with challenging long-held assumptions about China, particularly from Western contexts. In this sense, an underlying aim of this book is to counter some of the dominant views of China, and, in doing so, begin to surface more nuanced understandings of a country that is often portrayed in stereotypical ways, particularly where both education and AI technology are concerned. Furthermore, this focus on outsider perspectives offers an additional level of reflection on the relevance of studies of China to wider contexts: 'our' imaginaries of Chinese futures reveal much about ourselves, about how we understand the development of AI and the practice of education, and about where our aspirations and anxieties about the future lie.

Outline of chapters

Chapter 2 examines Chinese government policy related to AI, and its forming of authoritative imaginaries of state-controlled technologies, harnessed for the national agenda. This will focus on the *State Council's National Strategy for AI Development*[1] published in 2017, which has attracted wide interest and attention internationally, principally due to its explicit aims for global dominance in the field by 2030. However, aside from the various interpretations of geopolitical positioning and discussions of technological innovation that have accompanied the publication of the policy, little attention has been paid to the role of education in China's strategic plans for world-leading technical AI aptitude. This chapter therefore examines the less well-known *Action Plan for Artificial Intelligence Innovation in Colleges and Universities* published in 2018, in order to reveal significant plans for developing China's (higher) education system as the engine of broad societal reform towards AI, where institutions are positioned as training centres for new generations of technical expertise. Further education reforms will be shown to attempt to position universities as internationally recognised sites of AI power with world-leading research capacity in data-driven technologies. These policy visions are juxtaposed in the second half of the chapter with recent political history, to suggest a deep-seated theme of rejuvenation and 'overcoming backwardness', which still resonates in contemporary governance. This section will also outline examples of historical education reform, in order to suggest a continuity of placing Chinese education in service to the national agenda.

Following from the examination of the policy landscape, Chapter 3 explores the visions of AI circulating around the private sector, which frequently portray a vibrant entrepreneurial community of intensive technology development. Three key companies are outlined: New Oriental, Tomorrow Advancing Life (TAL), and Squirrel AI, which have emerged as large and influential education technology companies, and substantial players in the development of AI for education. Significantly, these companies developed substantial businesses and educational markets in the private after-school sector, thus designing their AI-driven products in ways to serve the particular needs of this population. The chapter will also examine, through the example of Sensetime – a company that developed data-driven technologies for computer vision, and is often identified as the world's first AI unicorn – the movement of China's 'big tech' companies into educational provision, often through the production of educational resources dedicated to AI training. As such, the private sector is suggested to be amassing significant authority in educational domains. Importantly, this chapter will also be grounded in an examination of historical contexts, focused on the origins of the private sector, and the development of private education provision in China. This will emphasise themes of precarity and innovation that continue to resonate in the contemporary visions of AI in education.

Chapter 4 returns to government policy, focusing specifically on the so-called 'double reduction' regulations which were published in the summer of 2021, and introduced a dramatic set of restrictions on private after-school tuition in China. While the policy was primarily directed at curbing the private education industry, as well as addressing a range of long-held concerns about the competitive education system in China, this chapter will suggest that the regulations have had a substantial impact on the development of AI. This impact will be traced by returning to the three key companies introduced in the previous chapter – New Oriental; TAL; and Squirrel AI – and examining the ways in which the policy has altered their approach to AI. The regulations will be shown to have radically transformed New Oriental's business, shifted TAL into a semi-government role to support other start-up companies with AI, and obliged Squirrel AI to pursue state school markets, as well as develop bespoke AI hardware. The chapter concludes by suggesting that the post-'double reduction' landscape is one in which AI development for education appears to have been pulled away from the private sector and closer to the government, further fuelling the imaginary of a data-driven technology that is able to be harnessed and managed by the state.

Chapter 5 examines the way relationships between AI and education have been shaped by geographical differences within China. This will begin with an examination of Zhongguancun (中关村), a long-established hub of technology development in northwest Beijing that has been incorporated into a broader vision of urban 'zones' of intensive entrepreneurial creativity and agglomeration. However, Zhongguancun will be shown to have distinct academic origins, and this will lead to the suggestion of a 'university AI power', in which higher education institutions are being imagined as core elements of future AI production through networks of government, private sector, and educational actors. Nevertheless, these arrangements will be shown to be clustering around urban areas, primarily in the eastern coastal provinces, and existing sites of higher socio-economic status and opportunity. His-torical contexts will be examined in the form of 'Special Economic Zones' (SEZs), which are suggested as precursors to the contemporary 'zones' of AI development, as areas of government experimentation with market reforms. Further, the more deep-seated historical divides between urban and rural areas in China, and the subsequent policies which have sought to address them, will be outlined as an underlying context for specific educational pro-jects, such as TAL's development of AI language learning for ethnic minor-ities in Sichuan province.

Chapter 6 examines a key dimension of the wider imaginaries of AI in the form of 'talent', a term often used to describe students and technology developers skilled in the techniques required for data-driven innovation. The first part of the chapter focuses on the domestic visions of AI skills generation, outlining plans for the cultivation of 'talent' right across the education spectrum in China, from special attention to PhD study, new high-profile 'AI major' undergraduate degrees, to a growing array of text-books and other educational resources being produced for school curricula by leading technology companies. This chapter will also extend the sugges-tions of 'university AI power', by examining the ways they are positioned as key elements in the vision of a 'talent pipeline' for the production of human capital that can drive government plans for economic transforma-tion. The second part of the chapter will examine some of the recent histor-ical uses of the term 'talent', specifically through attempts by the Chinese government to attract substantial populations of emigrant scientists and academics back to China, in order to contribute to the national agenda. The chapter culminates in an examination of the growing area of research attempting to measure 'national AI capacity' through statistical compar-isons and international ranking. This will be suggested to bolster instru-mental assumptions of 'AI talent', and the wider imaginaries of data-driven geopolitical rivalry.

Chapter 7 shifts the perspective from the wider flows of international 'AI talent' to a focus on the individual learner, and the extent to which data-driven platforms are being envisioned as technologies of 'personalisation' in education. Here, an imaginary of 'personalising' AI will be suggested, involving a valorisation of one-to-one pedagogical relationships, and the assumption of 'super-human' teaching abilities brought about by data-driven platforms. These visions will be shown to involve conflicting nar-ratives of the human teacher, as both increasingly redundant and valued for authentic teaching knowledge. The imaginary of personalisation will be contrasted with an examination of the 'knowledge space', a key functional aspect of educational AI platforms that renders topic areas into mathemat-ical representations of knowledge, and algorithmically controls subsequent student pathways. Such functioning will be suggested to have significant implications for ideas of student agency and subjectivity, for which the chapter will draw on concepts of educational purpose (Biesta 2009; 2015).

The final sections of the chapter will suggest three different notions of the 'self' emerging from Chinese political and social history: first, the 'divided self', and, second, the 'entrepreneurial self'. These themes will suggest some of the ways in which AI imaginaries might have taken hold in China, through the ways technologies appear to accommodate a distributed and conflicting Chinese self. Finally, a 'creative self' will be outlined to acknowledge long-standing calls for alternatives to China's focus on testing and rote learning, and suggest a groundwork from which alternative visions of education might shape the future of AI. As such, these perspectives suggest rich articulations of subjectivity and identity that are often erased in the imaginaries of 'personalising' AI.

Finally, chapter 8 offers a concise conclusion to the book. The first part summarises the use of sociotechnical imaginaries and social and political history as underlying theoretical frameworks across the book, emphasising the need for critical lenses through which to challenge the dominant narratives of AI innovation and disruption. The second part outlines the key contributions in each chapter, and underscores the central insights offered by the analytic combination of sociotechnical imaginaries and social and political history. The third and final section suggests future areas of research that might be approached through similar theoretical perspectives.

Note

1 The title of this policy is sometimes translated into English as the 'New Generation Artificial Intelligence Development Plan'.

References

Ball, S. (2013). *Foucault, power and education*. Abingdon, Oxon: Routledge.

Bareis, J., & Katzenbach, C. (2022). Talking AI into being: The narratives and imaginaries of national AI strategies and their performative politics. *Science, Technology, & Human Values*, 47(5), 855–881. https://doi.org/10.1177/01622439211030007

Bayne, S. (2015) What's the matter with 'technology-enhanced learning'?, *Learning, Media and Technology*, 40(1), 5–20. DOI: 10.1080/17439884.2014.915851

Biesta, G.J. (2009). Good education in an age of measurement: On the need to reconnect with the question of purpose in education. *Educational Assessment, Evaluation and Accountability*, 2(1), 33–46.

Biesta, G.J.J. (2015). What is education for? On good education, teacher judgement, and educational professionalism. *European Journal of Education*, 50(1), 75–87. https://doi.org/10.1111/ejed.12109

Brown, K. (2020). *China*. Cambridge: Polity Press

Chu, B. (2013). *Chinese whispers: Why everything you've heard about China is wrong*. London: Weidenfeld & Nicolson.

Garland, D. (2014). What is a "history of the present"? On Foucault's genealogies and their critical preconditions. *Punishment & Society*, 16(4), 365–384.

Guo, S. (2021). *The evolution of the Chinese internet: Creative visibility in the digital public*. Stanford: Stanford University Press.

Hamilton, E.C., and Friesen, N. (2013). Online Education: A Science and Technology Studies Perspective. *Canadian Journal of Learning and Technology* 39(2), 1-21

Jasanoff, S. (2015a). Future imperfect: Science, technology, and the imaginations of modernity. In S. Jasanoff & S-H. Kim (Eds.) *Dreamscapes of modernity: Sociotechnical imaginaries and the fabrication of power*. Chicago, IL: University of Chicago Press. 1–33

Jasanoff, S. (2015b). Imagined and invented worlds. In S. Jasanoff & S-H. Kim (Eds.) *Dreamscapes of modernity: Sociotechnical imaginaries and the fabrication of power*. Chicago, IL: University of Chicago Press. 321–342

Jasanoff, S., & Kim, S.-H. (2015). *Dreamscapes of modernity: Sociotechnical imaginaries and the fabrication of power*. Chicago, IL: University of Chicago Press.

Kleinoff, A., Yan, Y., Jun, J, Lee, S., Zhang, E., Tianshu, P., Fei, W., and Jinhua, G. (2011). *Deep China: the moral life of the person*. Berkley: The University of California Press.

Lin, C. (2006). *The transformation of Chinese socialism*. Durham, NC: Duke University Press.

Lin, C. (2013). *China and Global Capitalism: Reflections on Marxism, History, and Contemporary Politics*. New York: Palgrave MacMillan

Mager, A., & Katzenbach, C. (2021). Future imaginaries in the making and governing of digital technology: Multiple, contested, commodified. *New Media & Society*, 23(2), 223–236. https://doi.org/10.1177/1461444820929321

Morozov, E. (2013). *To save everything click here: Technology, solutionism and the urge to fix problems that don't exist*. London: Penguin.

Mosco, V. (2005). *The digital sublime (MIT Press): Myth, power, and cyberspace*, New ed. Cambridge, MA: MIT Press.

Vallor, S. (2021). Challenging and redrawing framings of technology to serve human flourishing and justice. *Edinburgh Innovations*. Available: https://edinburgh-innovations.ed.ac.uk/news/mobilising-the-intellectual-resources-of-the-arts-and-humanities

2 Policy, governance, and the state

This chapter examines the role of policy in shaping the relationships between artificial intelligence (AI) and education in China. Drawing from the concept of sociotechnical imaginaries introduced in the previous chapter, this analysis considers recent government policy related to AI as a particularly prominent vision of the future, in which both technology and education are assumed to play a fundamental role in state strategy. This constitutes a powerful vision of AI, in which both data-driven technologies and associated expertise can be governed and shaped towards national strategic priorities, developed and enhanced through the education system, and ultimately guided towards the establishment of a harmonious future economy. There are multiple dimensions to this vision, which will be examined across subsequent sections on national AI strategy in China, as well as specific policies on education reform. Two key policies will be analysed here: the *National Strategy for AI Development* (NSAID); the *Action Plan for Artificial Intelligence Innovation in Colleges and Universities* (APAICU). However, each of these policies is better understood within broader clusters of government regulation, and a much longer trajectory of positioning both science and technology and education as the motors of national development.

Crucially, this chapter will explore the ways the Chinese government, principally through policy directives, is seeking to liberate, harness, and manage the perceived economic power and geopolitical significance of AI. In introducing the concept of sociotechnical imaginaries, Jasanoff and Kim (2009) sought to foreground the influence of political power over science and technology development, which up until that time, they argued, had been given less attention within science and technology studies research. This chapter draws on this original contention to examine the ways the state, rather than the private sector, is seeking to control the AI narrative. Of course, the technology industry also holds significant sway over the vision of AI, and this will be examined in the subsequent chapter. Here, the emphasis will be on the state as a powerful actor in materialising technology futures

DOI: 10.4324/9781003375135-2

through the development of strategies and incentives, and, crucially, education. As Bareis and Katzenbach suggest, government AI strategies:

> constitute a powerful and peculiar hybrid of policy and discourse. They employ a prose of sober tech-policy, fierce national strategic positioning, and, at the same time, sketch bold visions of public goods and social order enabled through AI.
>
> (Bareis and Katzenbach 2022, p856)

While Mager and Katzenbach (2021) argue that industry now often dictates the imaginaries of AI futures, and thus performs the function of promising social order in ways previously undertaken by the state, the Chinese context suggests a more nuanced set of relations between public and private sectors. As will be examined below, Mager and Katzenbach's (2021) contention is certainly apparent in assumptions within government policy about the way AI functions, and the next chapter will further examine the powerful imaginaries emanating from China's entrepreneurial technology communities. Nevertheless, China's system of government, as the final section of this chapter will argue, is one that has long sought to manage and direct science and technology development for the national agenda, and this desire undoubtedly extends into contemporary AI strategy. The Chinese state is therefore a prominent and powerful actor in shaping the perception and expectation of AI, by 'combining powerful measures of issuing regulations and allocating resources with its own narratives and visions' (Bareis and Katzenbach 2022, p859). As Borup et al. further suggest, governments are able to 'guide activities, provide structure and legitimation, attract interest and foster investment' (Borup et al. 2006, p285–286), and China's AI policies provide the underlying vision for this action.

The final two sections of this chapter turn to recent political history in China, examining science and technology development, education reform, and changing modes of governance. The first of these sections outlines key events in China's transition from the Qing monarchy to the People's Republic of China (PRC), highlighting some of the causes underpinning subsequent ambitions for modernisation and development across the 20th century. These are suggested to offer additional ways of understanding the current policy-driven imaginaries of AI, as inflected by a sense of rejuvenation. In the final section, an examination of historical educational reform, principally after 1978, suggests a continuity of positioning education as the engine of economic transformation, and the means through which new kinds of expertise can be trained for national development. The rationale for accompanying the analysis of sociotechnical imaginaries with political history, as outlined in the introduction, is to suggest insight into the wider contexts through which visions of the future are formed.

National strategy and 'cold war' rivalry

In 2017 the State Council published the NSAID[1] (see State Council 2017), which is often cited as the key policy in China's recent focus on AI. A key passage in Section 3 of the policy specified three stages for achieving global leadership in the development of the technology:

> First, by 2020, the overall technology and application of AI will be in step with globally advanced levels... Second, by 2025, China will achieve major breakthroughs in basic theories for AI, such that some technologies and applications achieve a world-leading level and AI becomes the main driving force for China's industrial upgrading and economic transformation... Third, by 2030, China's AI theories, technologies, and applications should achieve world-leading levels, making China the world's primary AI innovation center, achieving visible results in intelligent economy and intelligent society applications, and laying an important foundation for becoming a leading innovation-style nation and an economic power.
>
> (State Council 2017) (in New America translation p5–6)

The policy thus represents an overt vision for AI ascendency, in which the technology is portrayed as transforming and enhancing China's industrial and economic development, and propelling the country into a position of international leadership. A range of assumptions underpin this imaginary, deriving not only from ideas about AI's ability to disrupt and revolutionise, but also a belief that such technologies can be shaped and managed by the state. The assumption that AI development is inevitable, and that it will exact unparalleled societal transformation, seems palpable in this policy projection, and these are themes mirrored in other analyses of the sociotechnical imaginaries of AI. Bareis and Katzenbach, for example, suggest the technology is 'depicted as a breakthrough, a revolution, almost a sublime force that lets society enter a new epoch in history' (Bareis and Katzenbach 2022, p864). For Mager and Katzenbach, the vision is that 'AI is inevitable and that it will fundamentally change how we live, communicate, work, and travel' (2021, p232). China's strategy thus seeks to 'establish AI as a given and massively disrupting technical development that will change society and politics fundamentally' (Bareis and Katzenbach 2022, p875). As such, the vision of AI-driven futures appears to be derived principally from industry:

> in governmental regulations and national AI strategies, the industry's narrative of inevitability of AI as a key technology that will necessarily become a central sociotechnical institution is the dominant imaginary.
>
> (Mager and Katzenbach 2021, p232)

However, while for Mager and Katzenbach (2021) this infers that technology companies are now the dominant actors in shaping visions of the future, particularly those future visions that suit their business interests, the Chinese context, as this book will argue, suggests a more powerful role for the state, and additional ways that political power can shape the sociotechnical imaginaries surrounding AI.

Certainly, there is an overt economic dimension to NSAID's vision of AI development. The policy is rather precise about future economic advantages, making particular emphasis of the 'AI industry gross output' at each stage of the strategy, for example, stating 'RMB 1 trillion (USD 150.8 billion)' for so-called 'core' AI, and 'RMB 10 trillion (USD 1.5 trillion)' for 'AI-related' industries (State Council 2017). This underscores a broader assumption that AI is inextricable from a coming economic transformation, perhaps most recognisable in the notion of a 'fourth industrial revolution' (see Schwab 2017). As Vicente and Dias-Trindade (2021) argue, the fourth industrial revolution itself is an imaginary premised upon the 'megatrends' of AI and other hyped technologies, in which ailing economies will undergo a straightforward technical fix. Furthermore, Schiølin's (2020) critique of the fourth industrial revolution imaginary also identifies the themes of 'inevitability' and 'epochalism': 'the feeling that the present is an unparalleled moment of historical significance' (2020, p552). This seems to align well with the bold plans in China's NSAID, which seems to conflate inevitable AI technologies with predestined economic transformation.

While assumptions about the ability of AI to transform the economy are a central aspect of the NSAID policy, there are also explicit visions of data-driven geopolitical ascendency, which have tended to merge with more established projections of a transpacific rivalry between the US and China. It is important here to consider the ways in which subsequent reporting and analysis of the NSAID appears to bolster the vision of global competition animated by national AI capabilities. Following the publication of the NSAID, the somewhat unambiguous aims seemed to induce a flurry of anxious media reporting and detailed policy analysis, particularly in the US. The policy was often cited in concerns over China's rising power (e.g. Knight 2017), in which AI development was frequently portrayed in terms of 'cold war' competition between the two countries (e.g. Doffman 2018; Thompson 2018; Borowska 2019; Heath 2020). With palpable concern, O'Meara's article in *Nature* suggested: '[t]he United States is ahead in terms of high-impact AI papers and people, but for how long?' (2019, p427). The NSAID also motivated much in the way of policy analysis, focusing on the potential geopolitical or economic significance of China's claims of AI ascendency (see Webster et al. 2017; Lee & Triolo 2017; Ding 2018; Roberts et al. 2021). The discourse around the NSAID appears, therefore, to have bolstered and intensified the imaginary of AI-driven dominance, rather than questioned the underlying assumptions about the capacity of the technology to straightforwardly transform and enhance national and economic development.

Furthermore, more long-standing predictions of a coming struggle and opposition between China and the US seem to be amplified through the visions for AI. Frederick Kempe, president of the Atlantic Council, a think tank based in Washington DC, described this vision clearly, suggesting that China is 'on track to take the commanding heights of AI' where 'the consequences could be historic in nature', for the reason that '[c]ountries that are most innovative and technologically advanced tend to dominate international relations' (Kempe 2019). As Knight further suggests, 'China's prowess in the field will help fortify its position as the dominant economic power in the world' (Knight 2017). Here, more established discourses of a 'gathering storm' (Mearsheimer 2010) between China and the US, or analyses of shifting regional power in the Asia-Pacific (e.g. Zhao 2015), seem to be rearticulated through the sociotechnical imaginary of AI, where the technology becomes the latest frontier in a tussle for power. Elevated by the publishing of NSAID, AI technology appears to take centre stage in this wider geopolitical rivalry, through the vision of a kind of talismanic technology, assumed to be capable of delivering huge economic benefits and unrivalled international influence. This politically charged imaginary of AI, inflected with a deep sense of conflict and competition, will surface again in subsequent chapters as a powerful projection of China's future.

As Bryson and Malikova (2021) demonstrate, there is little evidence to back up the claims of a straightforward binary opposition between AI development in the US and China, despite this being the dominant narrative in policy discourse. Ding and Costigan further suggest that 'national AI capability is such a fuzzy concept' (2019, p27), pointing out the various ways in which the development and governance of the technology transcends nation state boundaries. In a more recent analysis, Hine and Floridi (2022) critique the dominant portrayal of AI development as a fundamental clash between civilisations. Moreover, as Zhang et al. (2021) evidence through the results of a recent survey on the topic of challenges to the development of AI, 'US–China competition' was ranked the lowest out of 13 issues related to governance and ethics of the technology. That a sense of high-stakes competition between China and the US persists in the sociotechnical imaginaries of AI, as subsequent chapters will demonstrate, is a testament to its power and resilience as a vision of the future, as well as to the authority conferred on those that rehearse the narrative. Central to understanding the vision of an 'AI arms race' (Borowska 2019) is the extent to which the imaginary of an external threat motivates domestic policy on technology development. The NSAID itself might be considered a response to earlier US policy. For example, as Ding suggests, 'there is evidence that China is particularly attuned to US AI strategy, and sees it as a reference point for its own approach' (2018, p12). Further, as Allen and Kania (2017) contend, the NSAID was directly influenced by three reports published by the Obama administration in 2016, reports which highlighted, in particular, the economic significance of innovation in AI development. In turn, and following the publishing of China's

NSAID, the US have been accused of a 'lackluster' approach in comparison to China, necessitating a number of subsequent federal policies to prioritise AI research, including an executive order from the president and the establishment of a 'National AI Initiative Act' under the Trump administration in 2020 (Walch 2020). There are direct implications here for education. As will also be discussed below and in subsequent chapters, think tanks such as the Centre for Security and Emerging Technology in Washington DC have also published numerous reports that explicitly call for renewed education policy in the US as a response to China's AI strategy (e.g. Peterson et al. 2021).

While the NSAID offers a key example of policy imaginaries that appear to draw on wider assumptions about AI and its potential for economic transformation, it is crucial to situate the policy within China's wider strategising around technology, and education in particular. In this sense, the NSAID might be perceived as aligned with domestic, rather than necessarily international, strategy. As Ding (2018) suggests, the NSAID should be seen as the culmination of a range of recent policy work rather than an exclusive and isolated statement. Ding (2018) outlines a number of references to AI technology in Chinese government policy leading up to the publishing of the State Council's ambitions, including the 'Internet Plus' initiative, launched in 2015, and the subsequent 'Internet Plus and AI Three-Year Implementation Plan' published in 2016, as well as the '13th Five-Year Plan for Developing National Strategic and Emerging Industries' released in the same year. As Ding (2018) suggests, seen together, these planning documents evidence China's considerable ambitions in the field of AI development, but also a much longer project of capacity building than is evident from the NSAID alone. As Roberts et al. suggest, these policies 'indicate that there has been a conscious effort to develop and use AI in China for some time' (2021, p60). Ding (2018) also indicates some benefit to looking back further in terms of China's science and technology policy, outlining the significance of the 'National Medium- and Long-Term Plan (MLP) for the Development of Science and Technology' issued by the State Council in 2006, as well as the 'Made in China 2025' strategy launched in 2015 (also see Wübbeke et al. 2016). Notably, Wang suggests that 'Made in China 2025' was overtly positioned to 'catalyze China into a knowledge- and service-based economy' (2020, p100), perhaps precipitating the focus on AI. For Ding, these initiatives emphasise an 'indigenous innovation' (2018, p14) that is maintained in more recent AI policy, where independence from both foreign expertise and international supply chains are seen as crucial for technological self-sufficiency, a point underscored by Allen (2019) and Laskai and Toner (2019).

Crucially, then, situated within a wider cluster of policies focused on technology, the more recent AI strategy might be understood in terms of China's long-standing nationalist and developmentalist agendas (Lin 2006), as well as a deep-seated concern for self-reliance that underpins Chinese 20th-century politics (Kleinman et al. 2011) – this will be examined further below.

In this sense, the vision of AI in the NSAID might be perceived as aligning with core elements of China's (ongoing) project of socialist modernisation (Lin 2006), as much as it does with sociotechnical imaginaries of a data-driven economy. What unites Chinese politics and AI imaginaries here is the desire for control, the aspiration to manage China's progress through balancing nationalism, socialism, and developmentalism (Lin 2006), fused with the expectation of directing data-driven innovation towards state strategy. Perceived in this way, China's AI strategy appears as a projection of social order. However, as will be further elaborated here as well as across the following chapters, such attempts at centralised state control exist in tension with emerging regional hubs of AI governance, globalised markets of technology development, and the international trajectories of technical and entrepreneurial expertise, all of which agitate the inconsistencies and contradictions within the nationalist, socialist, and developmentalist framework.

The final dimension worth noting here is the assumption that AI technologies can be governed and controlled by the state, and thus tuned to national priorities. This is inferred rather directly in the NSAID, but also demonstrated in the wider cluster of policies that have attempted to incorporate AI development into the national agenda. However, importantly, it is also a vision of future AI governance that seems to resonate with long-held assumptions about China itself, as a one-party state, overtly hierarchical in both political and social structures. In other words, at least from outside perspectives, only China could envisage a future in which AI is managed through 'top-down' governance. For Ding, this is one of the 'myths' of China's AI strategy (if not the country itself): that the 'approach to AI is defined by its top-down and monolithic nature' (Ding 2018, p3). Rather, as Sheenan (2018) further suggests, the role of central government in AI development is to incentivise rather than direct. Roberts et al. are clear on this point, suggesting in reference to the NSAID (using the alternative acronym AIDP):

> the Plan is not meant to act as a centrally enacted initiative. The AIDP instead functions as a stamp of approval for de-risking and actively incentivising local projects that make use of AI. Recognising this point is important: the AIDP is an ambitious strategy set by the central government, but the actual innovation and transformation is expected to be driven by the private sector and local governments.
>
> (Roberts et al. 2021, p61)

This interpretation, not only challenges simplistic claims of a monolithic government straightforwardly overseeing an AI ascendency, but also opens up the possibility of a much more complex picture involving a range of competing actors, in the form of regional authorities and commercial, market-driven entities. The role of the private sector in particular will be examined in the subsequent chapter. However, the next section turns to the ways education is being envisioned as a central instrument of the government, and tuned towards the grand imaginary of an AI-driven state.

Education reform and the data-driven economy

As Bareis and Katzenbach contend:

> State actors possess the (legitimate) means to sketch future societal pathways and, at the same time, craft influential institutions that define the virtues and vices facilitated by novel technologies and culture.
>
> (Bareis and Katzenbach 2022, p859)

One of the central ways in which the Chinese government appears to be shaping the narrative of AI is through the incorporation of state education. Indeed, education features in two crucial ways, not only underpinning many of the ambitious claims for AI-driven futures, but also becoming the target for radical disruption and reform. In other words, not only is AI proposed as a novel form of technology with which to enhance pedagogical practices and 'personalise' student learning (examined specifically in Chapter 7), it is also positioned as a substantial new subject area itself for the development of future curricula. In this way, AI becomes thoroughly embedded in education, in the appearance of 'smart' classroom environments or personalising software platforms, as well as in the shaping of relevant knowledge, as new generations of students are assumed to require a foundational understanding of AI in order to function as members of a future data-driven economy and society.

Less prominent than the NSAID, the APAICU published in 2018, nevertheless, sets out similarly ambitious goals for the (higher) education sector in a three-stage proposal:

> establishing university infrastructures and curricula capable of adapting to AI, by a target date of 2020; enhancing research and development, as well as the workforce training in specific skills related to AI, by a target date of 2025; and finally, Chinese universities becoming global leaders in AI innovation, by a target date of 2030.
>
> (MEPRC 2018a)

Mirroring the three-step projection for AI ascendency in the NSAID, the APAICU thus appears to centralise higher education reform within the broader national imaginary. State development and educational reform, therefore, appear to go hand in hand. This is also suggested in the overt sense of nationalism throughout the APAICU, for example, calling for AI development to 'build a strong country of education, a strong country of science and technology, and a smart society' (MEPRC 2018a). Further, the development and utilisation of AI technology in the functioning of educational institutions as well as in the practices and activities of teaching and learning are also underscored. The APAICU states:

> accelerate the innovation and application of artificial intelligence in the field of education, use intelligent technology to support the innovation of talent training model, the reform of teaching methods, and the improvement of educational governance capabilities, and build an intelligent, networked, personalized and lifelong education system.
>
> (MEPRC 2018a)

Further significant details from the policy include aims for course and curricula development specific to AI, the creation of accompanying teaching materials, and the widening of participation in AI training opportunities. Particularly notable here are plans to position AI as a core disciplinary subject, alongside establishing 'first-level discipline' (MEPRC 2018a) examples, referring to designations of the best degree programme in a given subject in China. This consolidation of a specific discipline of 'AI' is significant, given criticism that training has been previously 'scattered' amongst other topics such as computer science and statistics (Xu et al. 2018). In addition, the APAICU emphasises interdisciplinary arrangements, termed 'AI + X', identifying combined degrees through which AI might be applied to 'mathematics, computer science, physics, biology, psychology, sociology, law and other disciplines' (MEPRC 2018a). These calls for education reform will be examined further in Chapter 6, in the context of developing AI expertise. Underpinning China's curricular development around AI are also calls for increased industry engagement and collaboration, and, as Chapters 3 and 6 will also discuss in detail, this constitutes substantial influence over the ways AI is defined and taught. Nevertheless, the APAICU appears to establish the parameters through which the private sector can become involved.

The APAICU also highlights a significant, yet often less acknowledged dimension of the broader geopolitical rivalry over AI dominance: extensive educational reform is positioned as a core necessity, and the underlying engine of a future data-driven economy. While much of the hyperbole around AI tends to focus on future data-driven economies and their potential transformative impact on society, such visions are too often premised upon the assumption of a radical overhaul of the underlying institutions which produce future citizens and expertise, that is, schools, colleges, and universities. Here the APAICU presents one example of an explicit vision for such a transformation, with, unsurprisingly, little reflection on how such changes might radically alter the project of education by seeming to place it in service to the demands of industry. As in the previous section, the policy discourse developed around China's strategic plans for AI appear to extend and reinforce this imaginary. Peterson et al.'s (2021) report is explicit about the formative role of education in an assumed transpacific rivalry, and portrays China's focus on educational reform as a strength of their AI strategy, as opposed to the more general focus on computer science found in the US (this is discussed further in Chapter 6). Elsewhere China's 'AI major' was reported as an explicit challenge to the US (Fang 2019). In this way, responses to China's plans for AI-driven education reform appear largely concerned with the potential strategic advantage gained through the production of a future workforce suitability skilled in the appropriate computer science techniques, rather than any anxiety for a potentially problematic datafication of the education sector. Peterson et al. (2021) suggest that 'China has benefited from its centralized, systematic approach to implementing AI education at all levels' and 'is well equipped to develop a robust, medium-term AI workforce pipeline' (2021, p34). In contrast, US education is largely portrayed as problematically decentralised, where the 'greater freedom and flexibility' of its model is suggested to manifest as a 'weakness when it comes to quickly leveling up the US workforce for AI and other emerging technologies' (Peterson et al. 2021, p35). The supposedly dire situation for the US is suggested to be further impacted where 'funding structures limit the ability for long-term planning' (Peterson et al. 2021, p35) and is 'exacerbated' by a system which 'relies on piecemeal or localized initiatives, especially when it comes to private sector involvement' (Peterson et al. 2021, p36). While Peterson et al. conclude that this doesn't necessarily place the US at a disadvantage – primarily due to the claim that '[a] greater degree of educational autonomy in the United States gives breathing room for experimentation, creativity, and innovation' (2021, p38–39) – the general thrust of the report seems to advocate, not only more centralised strategic governance of education, but also an extensive vocationalisation of the entire sector, justified unreservedly through a rationale of national economic competitiveness. This report is discussed further in Chapter 6, in the context of 'AI talent'.

In just the same way as the NSAID appears to have been framed as an external threat necessitating the overhaul of domestic AI policy in the US, so China's plans for education technology development seem to be similarly exploited as a justification for wholesale educational reform, specifically oriented towards the propagation of technical skills. It is worth noting here that research less focused on specific China-US relations paints a somewhat different picture. Recent metrics for so-called 'automation readiness' rank China (at the time of writing) as only 14th out of 25 countries in terms of its suitable educational policies, with the US achieving a slightly more respectable ninth (China Power Team 2020). Indeed, just as we have seen with the broader AI policy development previously, there are important ways to challenge prevailing assumptions about the impending role of AI in education in China, or, at the very least, offer an understanding of the educational context that isn't framed by visions of geopolitical rivalry, national security, and competition. In other words, there is valuable understanding to develop about the relationships between AI and education in China *on its own terms*. As with the previous section, this requires some acknowledgement of the historical educational contexts underpinning this latest call for reform, the cluster of other policies relating to the technical development of the sector, and an outline of the distributed, rather than necessarily centralised, arrangement of key actors and institutions involved in AI development.

One way to begin this examination is to highlight the wider policy landscape preceding the prominent examples discussed above, in order to surface the ways in which digital technologies have been positioned as key instruments of educational reform well before the current fascination with so-called 'AI'. One of the key terms here is 'informatization', used to refer to a broad range of technical enhancements to the education sector. The National Plan for Medium- and Long-Term Education Reform and Development 2020, launched in 2010, devotes an entire section to 'informatization', suggesting that '[a]ttention shall be given to the revolutionary impact of information technology on education development' (MEPRC 2010, p41). The policy further suggests:

> Quality resources and advanced technology shall be put into full use, operational mechanisms and management modes shall be renovated, and available resources shall be integrated, so that a sophisticated, efficient and practical online education infrastructure can be built.
> (MEPRC 2010, p41)

While the focus here appears to be on establishing digital infrastructure rather than AI systems specifically, the aims are clearly broad, and directed towards laying the groundwork for digital technologies becoming key elements of educational organisation and practice. This is taken forward more directly in the Ten-Year Plan for Education Informatization, issued in 2012 (see MEPRC 2012). Yan and Yang (2021) term this period 'Education Informatization 1.0', which was followed, perhaps unsurprisingly, by the Action Plan for 'Education Informatization 2.0' in 2018 (see MEPRC 2018b). This second version is clear about the connections with broader policy, suggesting 'informatization 2.0' as combined with 'the national "Internet +", big data, [and] new generation of artificial intelligence' (MEPRC 2018b). Thus, there is a clear sense of the Chinese government building its vision for AI-driven education through ongoing policy development, appearing to refine its directives and plans in response to subsequent technology developments (and, undoubtedly, private sector imaginaries), but also, arguably, asserting its authority over the AI narrative, and securing a place for educational institutions at the core of future transformations.

Following the launch of the previously discussed NSAID and APAICU, specific references to AI in relation to education have been more explicit. One notable example here is the 'Wisdom Education' initiative (where 'wisdom' may be better translated as 'smart') launched by the Ministry of Education in January 2019, involving the 'deep integration of big data, artificial intelligence, and education' (Yan and Yang 2021 p415). This sense of profound transformation engendered by data-driven technologies is underscored in an announcement in 2018 by Du Zhanyuan, Vice Minister of Education, who describes:

> changed human production, life and even the way of thinking and learning. The rapid development of artificial intelligence will bring more profound and even revolutionary changes to human social life, and will also bring unprecedented challenges and opportunities to educational reform.
>
> (Du 2018)

Importantly, one might also see here the ways in which the assumption of wider transformation in society is positioned as a justification for changes to the education sector. Here AI is framed as a rationale for (re)entrenching an economic model of education, in which the sector is positioned to serve the needs of a future technologised society in the form of human capital, rather than acknowledging the capacity of educational activity to critically challenge such a vision. Additionally significant here are Du's comments on the relationships between government and the private sector in realising the policy vision of AI-infused education:

> we should focus on mobilizing the forces of the whole society to promote the informatization of education, especially the role of the industry, rather than relying solely on the power of the government.
>
> (Du 2018)

Exemplifying the theme of government incentivisation discussed previously, this statement is indicative of a key feature of the governance of AI and education in China: the 'mobilisation' of private technology companies to drive technical development in the name of national development. Importantly, as this chapter argues, this is a potentially different configuration from the one in which the technology industry drives the sociotechnical imaginary of AI (e.g. Mager and Katzenbach 2021), and suggests a context in which the Chinese state is attempting to authorise and unleash the private sector in order to develop the technology, but is ultimately seeking to manage and control the future narrative. Moreover, that such AI governance is being articulated here within the context of educational reform attests to the foundational position into which state education is being situated. While Du further offers the analogy of 'two legs' suggesting 'the government and the market, the "invisible hand" and the "visible hand" work together' (2018), as will be discussed further across the following two chapters, the relationship between the state and the private sector might not be as egalitarian as portrayed here, particularly given the stringent regulations introduced in 2021 to drastically curb the influence of education companies (examined in detail in Chapter 4) as well as technology companies in general. Indeed,

Du's subsequent description of the relationships between the government, private sector, and education, while seeming to underscore the importance of educational institutions in driving forward government policy on AI, might also be read as inferring a hierarchy, in which the state functions to define both the narrative and direction of technology development: 'government policy support, enterprises participating in construction, and schools focusing on application' (Du 2018).

However, to examine the role of the state in more detail requires attention to political history in China, which suggests that educational reform, as well as the alignment of education with science and technology for the purposes of national development, might be perceived as a continuity across 20th-century China, rather than a sudden and unexpected initiative precipitated by recent policy on AI. Returning to Lin's 'nationalism, socialism, and developmentalism' (2006, p15) framework outlined in the introduction, it is important to acknowledge the ways education has often been positioned as a key engine of China's development. As the following section will argue, this is an important way of understanding how the current policy-driven visions of AI (and education) in China have been derived. Furthermore, as Bareis and Katzenbach suggest, AI strategies often constitute a 'denial of history', through promising transformations that 'will seemingly make everything different, an unforeseen revolution' (2022, p864). It therefore remains important to surface historical insights that might reground the sociotechnical imaginaries of AI, and offer ways of understanding how such ideas were made possible to envision.

Dreaming and humiliation

It is not just AI policy that appears to be envisioning the future. Rather, strategies relating to AI are better understood as positioned within a much broader government discourse under the current leadership of the Chinese Communist Party (CPC) that is focused on visions of China's rise. As Brown (2020) notes, the era of governance under president Xi Jinping (习近平) is distinguished in its discourse of ambition (here contrasted with the previous leadership of Hu Jintao – 胡锦涛):

> In the Hu era, the leadership had maintained a commitment to narrowly technocratic language, with next to no space for talking of ideals, aspirations, and expectations beyond those that could be captured in a statistic. For the new era, however, with its special qualities and the spectre of imminent revival, ideals and hopes, and dreams, could make a comeback.
>
> (Brown 2020, p150)

The notion of the 'China Dream' (中国梦), first mentioned at the very outset of Xi's party leadership (see Xi 2012), has become the foundational narrative of contemporary policy, and provides an important underlying context into which the relations between AI and education can be understood. As Brown (2020) suggests, the China Dream strategy can be viewed in terms of both an internal narrative of nationalism and a return to traditional Chinese values, as well as an external version, articulated through the highly publicised 'Belt and Road' (一带一路) initiative involving the establishing of global trade relations and infrastructure. Importantly, this 'China Dream' is underpinned by a discourse of rejuvenation – the term being 'one of the keywords of Xi-era discourse' (Brown 2020, p149), where both domestic and foreign policy are framed in terms of the restoration of China's standing in times past. While China's AI strategy might also be aligned with the broad policy discourse of the 'China Dream', it remains more important to examine the historical contexts through which such a vision is framed in terms of rejuvenation.

As Brown (2020) contends, much of China's politics and culture in the 20th and 21st centuries can be understood as deriving from the sense of national humiliation following the military defeats of the Opium Wars (1839–1841 and 1856–1860) and the first Sino-Japanese War (1894–1895). These events shocked an otherwise assured and confident Qing dynasty, and precipitated widespread calls for reform. Crucially, these military defeats were seen as resulting from China's lack of modernisation, and the subsequent period of reform in the early 20th century was not only heavily influenced by perceptions of the value of Western technology, but also focused on educational reform (Zhao 2016), and in particular the attempts to establish a science and technology curriculum (Yu et al. 2012). As Zhao (2016) notes, calls for modernisation in this period targeted traditional Confucian teaching as a symbol of China's backward ways and its inability to compete with Western powers, and gave rise to the establishment of a modern national school system in 1901, and the abolishment of the civil service examination in 1905. While these substantial events in China's history are only briefly outlined here, subsequent chapters will return to the early 20th century as offering important insights for the more contemporary interest in AI. For example, Chapter 3 will suggest links between beliefs in this period and the imaginary of China's explosive entrepreneurial interest in AI, while Chapter 6 will examine early examples of Chinese students travelling to the US to study 'Western' science, as a precursor to the substantial populations of 'AI talent' that now traverse the Pacific. Further, Chapter 7 will discuss the ways 'Western' technological prowess was misconstrued in this period, resulting in narrow, instrumental views of technology.

For now, 'overcoming backwardness' might be emphasised as a key theme emerging from this period, one which underpinned not only the early 20th-century reform period, but also the inception of the PRC in 1949. As Lin (2006) argues, the PRC was not simply driven by the ideologies of Maoist socialism, but was fundamentally shaped by a concern for defining national identity and establishing China's distinctiveness amongst the international community, primarily through industrial development, which was a direct response to the earlier notion of 'overcoming backwardness'. In this way, the CPC represents a continuation of earlier reform period beliefs, being concerned with national sovereignty secured through the development of modern science, technology, and industry. It is this deep-seated drive for 'overcoming backwardness' that extends back to China's military defeats in the late 19th century, which was continued through the focus on industrialisation after 1949, and which arguably continues into the contemporary discourse of 'rejuvenation' (Brown 2020). While it would be too simplistic to position this historical period of humiliation and reform as the ultimate explanatory narrative through which to understand contemporary China, it does establish the context from which the current discourse of 'rejuvenation' and the 'China Dream' can be understood (ibid), and thus the broader picture of national ambition that arguably motivates Chinese AI strategy. From such a perspective, the prognostications of China's AI-infused geopolitical dominance in the NSAID appear, not simply as a repetition of the promises of the data-driven fourth industrial revolution, but as a strategy that perhaps looks backward as much as forward, and frames technology development as a means of restoration as much as enhancement. Such a historical perspective is, of course, not intended to undermine or replace the sociotechnical imaginaries of AI suggested previously, but rather to augment and enrich them through an understanding of the contexts and convictions through which they are envisioned. Furthermore, it is important to emphasise that government policy, whether shaped by a sense of national rejuvenation or not, is only one dimension of the multifaceted vision of AI emerging in China, and the private sector in particular, as examined in the next chapter, offers another powerful narrative of data-driven Chinese futures.

Restoring education as the engine of reform

While a sense of national rejuvenation may inflect the policy-driven imaginaries of AI in China, the extent to which education is positioned as the engine of economic transformation also has precedents in recent political history. During the 'post-revolution' era – referring to the period after 1949 in which the CPC took power, Yu et al. suggest that the education system was almost entirely organised around national development, being 'directed to serve industrial, agricultural and the national defense sectors' (2012, p13). While this period lasted less than 20 years, it established an originary model of education as entirely in service to the planned economy, and socialist agenda of the state.

In the same period, the very beginnings of China's development of AI was initiated in the *Twelve-Year National Long-Term Outline for Science and*

Technology Development issued in 1956, which included the first Chinese reference to cybernetics, drawing influence from the Soviet Union (Wang 2018). However, just two years later the government launched the Great Leap Forward, which focused state resources on agriculture, industry, and steel production, thus effectively halting the development of computer science and cybernetics (ibid). The Cultural Revolution, between 1966 and 1976, thoroughly dismantled both science and technology development, and the entire education structure, in which the 'existing higher education system, including any Chinese, Western and Soviet traditions and practices, was nearly wiped out' (Yu et al. 2012, p14). When the Cultural Revolution was halted, and the new leadership of Deng Xiaoping (邓小平) initiated broad market-economy reforms, both education and science and technology were central to the reorganisational strategy. Within a year of his emergence as the paramount leader of China, Deng held the National Science Conference in March 1978, 'to restore and facilitate science and technology' (Wang 2018), and a just month later, delivered a speech at the 'National Conference on Education' to confirm that 'education must meet the requirements of our country's economic development' (Deng 2001). Thus, while research areas such as cybernetics were rekindled, eventually leading to the development of AI, education was also revived, and aligned with the 'market-based economic and policy mechanisms' (Yu et al. 2012, p15) that have since characterised China's governance. While this economic transformation continued over roughly the next 20 years in China, being depicted by some as 'the most spectacular in history' (see Chu 2013, p5), Brown (2020) stresses Deng's initial years as the foundation of later successes. In this way, Deng's prioritising of educational reform and the explicit positioning of education as a driving force of the economy have become foundational to the ways the government understand and oversee the sector.

Furthermore, as Yan and Yang (2021) claim, the current focus on 'informatization', 'wisdom education', and indeed data-driven AI can be traced back to Deng's speech on education in 1978, specifically through a reference to the use of media technologies for education, in which the paramount leader suggested:

> We must take steps to accelerate the development of modern media of education, including radio and television. Broadcasting offers an important means of developing education with greater, faster, better and more economical results, and we should take full advantage of it.
>
> (Deng 2001)

Here, media technologies of the time are framed as instruments through which education can be reformed as an engine of national development and economic growth, heralding the development of AI technologies to come, and firmly establishing the vision of efficiency and enhancement in the education system, wrought through new technological advances.

In addition, Deng's speech also framed educational transformation in ways that directly linked educational activity to the training of skilled workers, and, in turn, to national development:

> We must train workers with a high level of scientific and general knowledge and build a vast army of working-class intellectuals who are both 'red and expert'. Only then will we be able to master and advance modern science and culture and the new technologies and skills in every trade and profession. Only then will we be able to attain a productivity of labour higher than that under capitalism, [and] transform China into a modern and powerful socialist country.
>
> (Deng 2001)

This suggests a striking resemblance to aspects of China's current AI policy, which emphasises the production of AI 'talent' through education as a means to propel the national vision of economic transformation. This is examined further in Chapter 6, contextualised through a discussion of the renewal of overseas study following Deng's reforms – in other words, 'red experts' could also be educated abroad. Moreover, while Deng's speech in 1978 was primarily concerned with domestic development, given the systematic dismantling of education and science and technology over the previous decade, it also included notable ambitions for leadership on the world stage:

> If we are to catch up with and surpass the advanced countries in science and technology, we must improve not only the quality of our higher education but, first of all, that of our primary and secondary education. In other words, the primary and secondary school courses should be enriched with advanced scientific knowledge, presented in ways the pupils at these levels can understand.

Crucially, it is education that is positioned as the means through which such ascendency might be achieved. This offers a significant precedent, not only for the plans to align higher education with AI development examined previously in the APAICU, but also for the movement to produce school-level AI curricular and resources, examined in more detail in Chapter 6. As such, a brief examination of recent educational reform in China reveals a concerted interest in situating education at the very core of state strategy, as an engine of economic transformation, and as the means to bolster national development and geopolitical positioning, establishing a pattern that appears to be continued in contemporary AI policy.

Concluding remarks

This chapter examined the governance of AI and education, primarily through an analysis of policy, and a suggestion of the ways in which such discourse contributes to a wider sociotechnical imaginary of data-driven transformation. Two policies were examined: the NSAID, and the APAICU. The first policy envisions AI as driving national development and a future data-driven economy, as well as precipitating China's geopolitical dominance. However, such an imaginary appears to have been bolstered by a vast range of media reporting and analysis, which has tended to shape the narrative towards one of cold war rivalry with the US. The second policy specifies substantial plans for education reform, in order to develop AI curricula, train new kinds of expertise, and situate colleges and universities as the engine of wider data-driven economic transformations. However, such education policy also appears to have become the site of tense competition between China and the US.

The second half of the chapter shifted to perspectives from political history, offering ways of grounding the proliferating visions of a transpacific AI arms race. First, China's 20th century was briefly outlined in direct comparison to the contemporary policy discourse of 'China Dream', in order to suggest a deep-seated desire for rejuvenation and 'overcoming backwardness', deriving from encounters with Western technologies. Second, selected periods of educational reform were outlined in order to suggest a continuity of placing Chinese education in service to the national agenda, and driving economic development. Specifically, Deng Xiaoping's speech on education in 1978 was emphasised as a key moment in establishing this view. Establishing education as a key driver of national development still largely defines the way the sector is governed today.

As a final reflection, following Mager and Katzenbach's (2021) contention that the technology industry has now come to the fore in dictating sociotechnical imaginaries, particularly around AI, this chapter has argued that in the Chinese context, the state still appears to hold significant sway over the future. The long-standing theme of rejuvenation can be understood to shape the current policy-driven sociotechnical imaginary of AI. This suggests an understanding of the ambitions for AI ascendency in China's national strategy, not simply as deriving from assumptions about the capacity of the technology to bring about instrumental economic gains, but also as a means to address a deep-seated sense of humiliation in the country's political history. Further, that state education is being positioned as the engine of data-driven transformation further demonstrates the ways the government is attempting to shape the sociotechnical imaginary of AI, principally by foregrounding standardised curricula, but also through university research institutes. Furthermore, the policy visions examined here are highly performative, in the sense that they guide and incentivise the activities of regional governments and the private sector, provide structure for and legitimise subsequent action, offer and encourage investment, as well as attract wider stakeholder and public interest to the cause.

Note

1 Also sometimes translated as the '*New Generation Artificial Intelligence Develop-ment Plan*'.

References

Allen, G.C. (2019). Understanding China's AI strategy clues to Chinese strategic thinking on artificial intelligence and national security. *Centre for New American Security*. Available: https://www.cnas.org/publications/reports/understanding-chinas-ai-strategy

Allen, G.C., & Kania, E.B. (2017). China is using America's own plan to dominate the future of artificial intelligence. *Foreign Policy*. 08 September, 2017. Accessed 4th August 2021. http://foreignpolicy.com/2017/09/08/china-is-using-americas-own-plan-to-dominate-the-future-of-artificial-intelligence/

Bareis, J., & Katzenbach, C. (2022). Talking AI into being: The narratives and imaginaries of national AI strategies and their performative politics. *Science, Technology, & Human Values*, *47*(5), 855–881. https://doi.org/10.1177/01622439211030007

Borowska, K. (2019). The AI arms race means we need AI ethics. *Forbes*. Accessed 23 April 2019. https://www.forbes.com/sites/kasiaborowska/2019/01/22/the-ai-arms-race-means-we-need-ai-ethics/#223f914867a0

Borup, M., Brown, N., Konrad, K. & Van Lente, H. (2006). The sociology of expectations in science and technology, *Technology Analysis & Strategic Management*, 18:3-4, 285-298, DOI: 10.1080/09537320600777002

Brown, K. (2020). *China*. Cambridge: Polity Press

Bryson, J.J., & Malikova, H. (2021). Is There an AI Cold War? *Global Perspectives*, 2(1), 24803. https://doi.org/10.1525/gp.2021.24803

China Power Team. (2020). Is China ready for intelligent automation? *China Power*. 19 October 2018. Updated 25 August 2020. Accessed 02 July 2021. https://chinapower.csis.org/china-intelligent-automation/

Chu, B. (2013). Chinese whispers: Why everything you've heard about China is wrong. London: Weidenfeld & Nicolson.

Deng, X. (2001). Speech at the national conference on education, 22nd April 1978. In *Selected works of Deng Xiaoping* [in Chinese]. People's Education Press. https://dengxiaopingworks.wordpress.com/2013/02/25/speech-at-the-national-conference-on-education/

Ding, J. (2018). Deciphering China's AI Dream: The context, components, capabilities, and consequences of China's strategy to lead the world in AI. *Future of Humanity Institute Report*. https://www.fhi.ox.ac.uk/wp-content/uploads/Deciphering_Chinas_AI-Dream.pdf

Ding, J., & Costigan, J. (2019). "Interview" in AI policy and China: Realities of state-led development, G. Webster (Ed.). Stanford-New America Digichina Project Special Report No. 1. p. 27. https://newamerica.org/documents/4353/DigiChina-AI-report-20191029.pdf

Doffman, Z. (2018). As the AI cold war looms, has time finally been called on China's spy industry? *Forbes*. 22 December 2018. Available: https://www.forbes.com/sites/zakdoffman/2018/12/22/as-the-ai-cold-war-looms-has-time-finally-been-called-on-chinas-spy-industry/?sh=75fe365f30a6

Du, Z. (2018). Deputy minister of Education Du Zhanyuan: Artificial intelligence and future educational reform [in Chinese]. *360doc* http://www.360doc.com/content/18/0527/10/30898787_757374036.shtml

Fang, A. (2019). Chinese colleges to offer AI major in challenge to US. *Nikkei Asian Review.* https://asia.nikkei.com/Business/China-tech/Chinese-colleges-to-offer-AI-major-in-challenge-to-US Accessed 21 August 2021

Heath, R. (2020). Artificial intelligence cold war on the horizon. *Global Translations.* 16th October 2020. Available: https://www.politico.com/news/2020/10/16/artificial-intelligence-cold-war-on-the-horizon-429714

Hine, E., & Floridi, L. (2022). Artificial intelligence with American values and Chinese characteristics: a comparative analysis of American and Chinese governmental AI policies. *AI & Soci*ety. https://doi.org/10.1007/s00146-022-01499-8

Jasanoff, S., & Kim, S-H. (2009). Containing the atom: Sociotechnical imaginaries and nuclear power in the United States and South Korea. *Minerva*, 47, 119–146.

Kempe, F. (2019). The US is falling behind China in crucial race for AI dominance. *CNBC.* Accessed 20 April 2019. https://www.cnbc.com/2019/01/25/chinas-upper-hand-in-ai-race- could-be-a-devastating-blow-to-the-west.html

Kleinman, A., Yan, Y., Jun, J, Lee, S., Zhang, E., Tianshu, P., Fei, W., and Jinhua, G. (2011). *Deep China: the moral life of the person.* Berkley: The University of California Press.

Knight, W. (2017). China's AI awakening. *MIT Technology Review.* Accessed 9 May 2019. https://www.technologyreview.com/s/609038/chinas-ai-awakening/

Laskai, L., & Toner, H. (2019). Can China grow its own AI tech base? In G. Webster (Ed.) *AI Policy and China: Realities of State-Led Development.* Stanford-New America Digichina Project Special Report No. 1. pp. 3–8. https://newamerica.org/documents/4353/DigiChina-AI-report-20191029.pdf

Lee, K-F., & Triolo, P. (2017). China's artificial intelligence revolution: Understanding Beijing's structural advantages. *Sinovation Ventures Report, Eurasia Group.* Accessed 2 June 2019. https://www.eurasiagroup.net/files/upload/China_Embraces_AI.pdf

Lin, C. (2006). *The transformation of Chinese socialism.* Durham, NC: Duke University Press.

Mager, A., & Katzenbach, C. (2021). Future imaginaries in the making and governing of digital technology: Multiple, contested, commodified. New Media & Society, 23(2), 223–236. https://doi.org/10.1177/1461444820929321

Mearsheimer, J.J. (2010). The gathering storm: China's challenge to US power in Asia. *Chinese Journal of International Politics,* 3(4), 381–396. https://doi.org/10.1093/cjip/poq016

MEPRC [Ministry of Education of the People's Republic of China]. (2010). *National plan for medium and long-term education reform and development.* UNESCO Translation available: https://uil.unesco.org/i/doc/lifelong-learning/policies/china-outline-of-chinas-national-plan-for-medium-and-long-term-education-reform-and-development-2010-2020.pdf

MEPRC [Ministry of Education of the People's Republic of China]. (2012). *Ten-year development plan for education informatization* (2011–2020) [in Chinese]. http://old.moe.gov.cn/publicfiles/business/htmlfiles/moe/s5892/201203/133322.html

MEPRC [Ministry of Education of the People's Republic of China]. (2018a). *Action Plan for Artificial Intelligence Innovation in Colleges and Universities.* Accessed 20 April 2019. http://www.moe.gov.cn/srcsite/A16/s7062/201804/t20180410_332722.html

MEPRC [Ministry of Education of the People's Republic of China] (2018b). *Education informatization 2.0 action plan* [in Chinese] http://www.moe.gov.cn/srcsite/A16/s3342/201804/t20180425_334188.html

O'Meara, S. (2019). Will China lead the world in AI by 2030? *Nature*, 572, 427–428. 22nd August. https://media.nature.com/original/magazine-assets/d41586-019-02360-7/d41586-019-02360-7.pdf

Peterson, D., Goode, K., & Gehlhaus, D. (2021). AI Education in China and the United States: A comparative assessment. CSET [Center for Security and Emerging Technology] Issue Brief. September 2021. Available: https://cset.georgetown.edu/wp-content/uploads/CSET-AI-Education-in-China-and-the-United-States-1.pdf

Roberts, H., Cowls, J., Morley, J., Taddeo, M., Wang, V., & Floridi, L. (2021). The Chinese approach to artificial intelligence: an analysis of policy, ethics, and regulation. *AI & Society*, 36, 59–77. https://doi.org/10.1007/s00146-020-00992-2

Schiølin, K. (2020). Revolutionary dreams: Future essentialism and the sociotechnical imaginary of the fourth industrial revolution in Denmark. *Social Studies of Science*, 50(4), 542–566. https://doi.org/10.1177/0306312719867768

Schwab, K. (2017). *The Fourth Industrial Revolution*. London: Portfolio Penguin.

State Council. (2017). *New generation artificial intelligence development plan*. July 2017. Accessed 27 April 2019. http://www.gov.cn/zhengce/content/2017-07/20/content_5211996.htm

***translation from New America here: https://na-production.s3.amazonaws.com/documents/translation-fulltext-8.1.17.pdf https://d1y8sb8igg2f8e.cloudfront.net/documents/translation-fulltext-8.1.17.pdf

Thompson, N. (2018). The AI cold war that threatens us all. *Wired*. Accessed September 3 2019. https://www.wired.com/story/ai-cold-war-china-could-doom-us-all/

Vicente, P. N., & Dias-Trindade, S. (2021). Reframing sociotechnical imaginaries: The case of the Fourth Industrial Revolution. *Public Understanding of Science*, 30(6), 708–723. https://doi.org/10.1177/09636625211013513

Walch, F. (2020). Why the race for AI dominance is more global than you think. *Forbes*. 9th February 2020. Available; https://www.forbes.com/sites/cognitiveworld/2020/02/09/why-the-race-for-ai-dominance-is-more-global-than-you-think/#140b211121ff

Wang, J. (2018). *The early history of artificial intelligence in China (1950s–1980s)*. Paper presented in the Graduate Student Workshop at 2018 Annual Meeting of the Society for the History of Technology (SHOT), St. Louis, MO. Accessed 15 September 2019. http://wangjieshu.com/2018/10/17/history_of_ai_in_china/

Wang, X. (2020). *Blockchain chicken farm, and other stories of tech in China's countryside*. New York: FSG Originals X Logic.

Webster, G., Creemers, R., Triolo, P., & Kania, E. (2017). China's plan to 'lead' in AI: Purpose, prospects, and problems. *New America*. Accessed 2 August 2019. https://www.newamerica.org/cybersecurity-initiative/blog/chinas-plan-lead-ai-purpose-prospects-and-problems/

Wübbeke, J., Meissner, M., Zenglein, M.J., Ives, J., & Conrad, B. (2016). MADE IN CHINA 2025. The making of a high-tech superpower and consequences for industrial countries. MERICS [Mercator Institute for China Studies] Report No. 2 December 2016. Available: https://www.merics.org/sites/default/files/2020-04/Made%20in%20China%202025.pdf

Xi, J. (2012). *The people's wish for a good life is our goal*. 15th November 2012, in The Governance of China, Vol. 1 (Beijing: Foreign Languages Press, 2014), 3.

Xu, D., L. He, and W. Zhao. 2018. The current situation of artificial intelligence education in domestic universities: it is imperative to establish a first-level discipline and strengthen the integration of production and education. The Paper. Accessed September 23 2019. https://www.thepaper.cn/newsDetail_forward_2087214

Yan (闫守轩), S., & Yang (杨运), Y. (2021). Education Informatization 2.0 in China: Motivation, framework, and vision. *ECNU Review of Education*, *4*(2), 410–428. https://doi.org/10.1177/2096531120944929

Yu, K., Stith, A.L., Liu, L., & Chen, H. (2012). *Tertiary Education at a Glance: China*. Rotterdam: Sense Publishers.

Zhang, B., Anderljung, M., Kahn, L., Dreksler, N., Horowitz, M.C., & Dafoe, A. (2021). Ethics and governance of artificial intelligence: Evidence from a survey of machine learning researchers. *Journal of Artificial Intelligence Research*, 71, 591–666.

Zhao, G. (2016). China's historical encounter with the West and Modern Chinese education. In G. Zhao & Z. Deng (Eds.) *Re-envisioning Chinese education: The meaning of person-making in a new age*. Abingdon: Routledge. pp. 13–33.

Zhao, S. (2015). A new model of big power relations? China–US strategic rivalry and balance of power in the Asia-Pacific. *Journal of Contemporary China*, 24(93), 377–397. https://doi.org/10.1080/10670564.2014.953808

3 Innovation, entrepreneurialism, and private enterprise

This chapter is concerned with examining the ways in which the private sector is shaping the relationships between education and artificial intelligence (AI) in China. This begins with an overview of some of the key imaginaries that surround the use of AI in education in China, focusing predominantly on accounts from outside of the country, which tend to depict a vibrant industry, within which businesses and start-up companies are able to take advantage of a unique national context. This includes accounts of China's large population, often interpreted in terms of valuable troves of data, within a society and government less concerned with notions of privacy than their Western counterparts. Chinese education, particularly private after-school provision, is thus frequently portrayed, in terms of not only a 'market' of willing students, underpinned by a cultural and parental pressure to value intensive study, but also a marketplace of viable businesses worthy of international investment.

This is followed by an examination of three of the most prominent companies involved in developing AI for education in China, revealing the establishment of substantial businesses that have emerged as highly influential both domestically and internationally. However, significantly, the AI developed by these companies is shown to derive from the commercial practices of the sizeable after-school tuition market in China, which puts a very particular emphasis on exam preparation and language learning. This has conditioned their AI products to be focused on standardised learning and persistent testing, which has also made their services popular with families looking to improve their children's achievements in China's highly competitive educational landscape. Alongside businesses focused exclusively on education, there is also a significant trend for China's established 'big tech' companies to shift into educational provision, and in the process become new kinds of educational authorities. This will be suggested to be another dimension of the imaginary of AI-infused education, in which technical systems and expertise developed in a specific area can be reconfigured into educational products and expertise. Such strategies can also be understood as attempts by already successful companies to develop benevolent aspects to their business, in part to remain within favourable political foci.

DOI: 10.4324/9781003375135-3

While these accounts suggest a powerful role for commercial entities in the development of AI for education in China, the final part of the chapter will examine the historical context of privatisation, as a way of deepening the understanding of the relationships between the Chinese state and private enterprise. This will suggest a more complex picture than the simplistic accounts of private sector innovation battling with government regulation, as often appears to underpin the discourse around technology development elsewhere, particularly in the US. With specific reference to the development of technology, Guo describes 'intricate dynamics between the state, semi-official forces, and non-state actors' that 'have jointly catalysed China's technology modernisation process' (2021, p3), and it is through similar relationships that the development of AI and education might be understood. Rather than portraying the state and the private sector as rigid elements that interact, this exploration will suggest factors that are co-constitutive of one another. In other words, this section of the chapter aims to surface the ways in which the state has shaped the private sector, and, correspondingly, the ways business interests have moulded and influenced China's governance.

The primary historical concern for this book is the rise of the private education sector during the 1980s and 1990s; however, as will be discussed below, the underlying context for this entrepreneurial enterprise is the wider shift from an industrial to a technological state (as well as from monarchy to republic). This focus continues the historical perspectives foregrounded in the previous chapter with respect to policy, and emphasises the need to contextualise contemporary AI development through an understanding of the ways in which privatisation formed and evolved in modern times, both in a general sense and with regard to education specifically. What is particularly interesting about China is that privatisation effectively disappeared during the first 30 years of the People's Republic of China (PRC), and the particular manner of its relatively recent revival provides crucial insights for a more general understanding of contemporary education and its relations with technology.

AlphaGo and China's 'Sputnik Moment' for AI

Offering a notable alternative to the policy-induced visions of an AI arms race discussed in the previous chapter, a series of highly publicised matches of the board game Go are often cited as a foundational moment in China's development of the technology (Lee 2018; Roberts et al. 2021). These matches involved professional players Lee Sedol (in March 2016) and Ke Jie (in May 2017), who were both defeated by the artificial neural network-based computer programme 'AlphaGo'. In particular, prominent computer scientist and technology executive Kai-Fu Lee describes these defeats as a 'Sputnik Moment' (Lee 2018, p3) for China's AI development, which 'lit a fire under the Chinese technology community that has been burning ever since' (2018, p3). As such, while nevertheless maintaining the cold war analogy (referring to the supposed motivational impact of Russian aerospace engineering in its capacity to ignite US involvement in the resulting 'space race'), Lee (ibid) establishes an alternative origin story for the private sector interest in AI, in which the victories of AlphaGo, rather than any overt geopolitical positioning, become the key inspiration for technology development. While Bory (2019) provides a more in-depth analysis of the narratives of AI surfaced through AlphaGo (as well as IBM's 'Deep Blue' chess-playing computer of the late 1990s), it is important here to emphasise the influence of Lee Sedol and Ke Jie's defeats on the sociotechnical imaginary emerging from the Chinese technology community. Ostensibly, AI, in the form of AlphaGo, had triumphed over a game with deep roots in Chinese history, culture, arts, and scholarship. While Go (or 围棋 – 'weiqi' – in Chinese) is widely appreciated for its extreme complexity, it holds a special place in Chinese (as well as Korean and Japanese) consciousness as an ancient game of the highest intellectual merit. That two of the world's best Go players (Lee Sedol is Korean, and Ke Jie Chinese) were beaten by AI technology thus had the effect of destabilising long-held beliefs in the superiority of the game itself. Furthermore, that the triumphant AlphaGo was developed by the UK-based company DeepMind Technologies, which was acquired by the US-based Google in 2014 (see Bray 2014), appeared to represent, at least from the Chinese perspective, Western technology gaining mastery over tradition, in ways that arguably connect back to early 20th-century encounters between the East and the West. In this way, the rationale of 'overcoming backwardness' that characterised this period (Zhao 2016; Brown 2020), and underpinned the establishment of the PRC (Lin 2006), as discussed in the previous chapter, appeared to resurface through AI's apparent mastery over the game of Go, rousing China's tech entrepreneurs into new modes of productivity.

As such, the sociotechnical imaginaries of AI emerging from China might be understood, not as exclusively deriving from the promises of innovative technical enhancements, but also modulated by a deep-seated concern for deficient technological progress.

Mass-scale solutions and explosive 'ed tech'

Against a backdrop of dramatic private sector innovation in China, regularly depicted in terms of vibrant and creative entrepreneurial cultures, and the almost mythical founding of 'big tech' companies such as Baidu, Tencent, and Alibaba (e.g. Lee 2018), the production of AI for education is frequently portrayed in similarly vivid terms. China is described as 'the most cutthroat competitive environment on the planet' where 'speed is essential … and competitors will stop at nothing to win a new market' (Lee 2018, p15). This discourse is constitutive of an important array of imaginaries that promote the Chinese context for AI-driven education as a site of rampant innovation, often with inferences of competitive advantage.

One of the central visions of Chinese AI for education involves a sense of scaled and prolific industry. As discussed in the introduction to this book, Lee contends that 'China appears poised to leapfrog the United States in education AI' (Lee 2018, p124), precisely due to the magnitude of the Chinese technology community, and the fervour through which start-ups and entrepreneurs are toiling. The sense of scale is further emphasised in the assertion that 'China leads the way in mass-scale e-learning solutions that combine human teachers and AI' (Lee 2021). However, this prolific private sector activity is also often framed in terms of an unprecedented level of government support (Lee 2018), through which companies working on education in particular are given additional incentives, such as tax breaks, making them attractive targets for investors (Hao 2019). This contributes to a general imaginary that China is operating on inequitable terms with other countries where the state is less inclined to intervene in the fortunes of the private sector, in particular in the US. This is perhaps the assumption through which Hao describes China as a country engaged in a 'grand experiment' (2019) with AI education, further accentuating the sense in which technological development is being undertaken at an unprecedented scale. Hao further conveys a sense of drama in China's approach, in which both the scale and speed of technical development are portrayed as uniquely Chinese attributes:

> While academics have puzzled over best practices, China hasn't waited around. In the last few years, the country's investment in AI-enabled teaching and learning has exploded. Tech giants, startups, and education incumbents have all jumped in. Tens of millions of students now use some form of AI to learn.... It's the world's biggest experiment on AI in education, and no one can predict the outcome.

Encompassed in the sense of scale are therefore also assumptions of explosive entrepreneurial activity, involving multiple actors boosted by government support. The sense of urgency here is another key aspect of the imaginaries around Chinese AI, in which China is inferred to be an undisputed leader in the adoption and acceptance of the technology, and, by extension, Western countries have been left behind, too contemplative to seize the opportunity. This is often a vision extolled in the US, which, as discussed in the previous chapter, is often framed as China's fundamental competitor in the newly articulated 'cold war' for AI supremacy. This is a key theme, and subsequent chapters will provide further examples of imaginaries about Chinese AI that, often through accounts of China's technical proficiency, seem intent on rousing US policy-makers to follow suit. Depictions of the way China's education system is being fine-tuned for AI dominance in Chapter 6 are one such example. While China's assumed scale is often, therefore, portrayed as intimidating, and as a motivation to measure up, it is also assumed to align with the necessary demands of AI development, in the form of the accumulation of data. Hao suggests:

> Chinese entrepreneurs have masses of data at their disposal to train and refine their algorithms. The population is vast, people's views on data privacy are much more lax than in the West (especially if they can get coveted benefits like academic performance in return).
>
> (Hao 2019)

This is a typical example of the way China is envisioned as a domain of abundant data, through which AI systems can be trained for educational applications like nowhere else in the world, affording the country a distinct advantage over those more discerning about issues such as privacy. Lee describes data as a '"natural resource" of China's tech world' (2018, p16). Scale, rapid development, and the abundance of data seem to combine to depict China as a spectacle of intensive AI development and deployment, as well as unadulterated technology adoption. Claims of 60 new AI companies establishing themselves in China's private market in 2018 alone (see Beard 2020) seem to further imply an alarming acceptance of data-driven educational activity. Such visions of pervasive AI in China's education seem inclined to portray the country as 'other', an intrinsically different reality, embracing questionable technology through impenetrable cultural differences. Further implied here is the assumption of a Chinese population 'obsessed with education' (Chu 2013, p5), and willing to overlook concerns about privacy for the chance to improve their outcomes.

Significantly, Chinese companies developing AI for education are often the subject of detailed accounts in financial news outlets and investment media, demonstrating the ways they are envisioned as productive businesses, able to thrive in China's educational landscape, as well as attract international financiers and venture capitalists. Such visions are also underpinned by an emphasis on scale. A central dimension of this discourse around AI stresses the underlying notion of 'market', particularly where private after-school education constitutes the principal area in which software products and services are deployed. The private education sector is thus often described in terms of its overall worth, at least before the regulations discussed in the following chapter – by some estimates $300 billion (Ni 2021). Qi (2020) valued China's 'Ed Tech' market at ¥453.8 billion (roughly $66 billion) in 2020. Further, China is frequently claimed to be the 'largest EdTech market' (Qi 2020), with its substantial population being framed as substantial pool of potential consumers. Qi (2020) suggests, 'the number of online educational users in China reached 423 million as of March 2020, an increase of 110.2% from the end of 2018'. Thus, China's 'market' is confirmed as both large and expanding, in ways that make investments in private education companies appear appealing. Indeed, Chinese AI education companies are often included in investment listings, defined purely in terms of their economic dimensions (e.g. Tracxn 2022). This interest in financial viability is an important part of the ways imaginaries about China's AI-driven education become stabilised around economic renditions of education. As Ding (2018) notes, Chinese AI start-ups became the target of huge international investments in 2016, particularly from the US, while education companies, such as Squirrel AI, discussed further below, are frequently ranked amongst the most productive (Deloitte 2019). As Yu further contends, '[t]he private education sector has become one of China's major service industries that investors, both foreign and domestic, see as particularly promising' (2019, p1). As such, the development and maintenance of markets of users, and ultimately profitability, would appear to be fundamentally necessary priorities for such companies, as distinct from purely educational ideals. This may not make private education companies entirely distinct from state institutions, which are undoubtedly also driven by the need to remain financially feasible. However, the extent to which AI education companies appear to be heavily engaged in global investment activity, as will be explored further below, seems to place them in a different category of financial accountability.

Importantly, however, such reports also appear concerned with the extent to which China's fertile markets of AI-infused education might be seen as deriving from a unique Chinese culture. Qi's (2020) report contends that with:

> hundreds of EdTech start-ups across China, global markets should realize the innovative ways in which China utilizes digital tools to enhance students' education in China. This phenomenon also stems from cultural factors, as Chinese society has always vigorously upheld education as one of its core cultural and social values. It is important to make a note of how China has integrated this value with the realm of technology and innovation.

The proliferation of AI for education is thus portrayed as particularly Chinese, and successful in a way that may not be possible elsewhere. In a sense, this aligns with suggestions of China's fundamental dissimilarity with other national contexts, however in a way that seems more concerned with assessing the viability of foreign investments. Hao's description of Chinese specificity is perhaps more direct: 'academic competition in China is fierce ... Parents willingly pay for tutoring or anything else that helps their children get ahead' (Hao 2019). This, in a way, encapsulates the vision of AI-driven education in China as a 'market', one populated by huge numbers of potential students who are heavily inclined to consume AI products, motivated by intensive competition, and financed by concerned families.

Across these visions of China's AI education industry, therefore, a range of assumptions seem to underpin a general expectation of vibrancy and success. The deployment of AI 'works' in China like nowhere else, one is led to assume, not only due to the proliferation of technology entrepreneurs, but also because of a conducive 'market' of learners, keen to consume the various data-driven educational products on offer. The next section turns to examining this 'market' in more detail, specifically in terms of the development of prominent companies.

'Big players' in AI education

While there is a broad range of companies involved in developing AI technologies for education in China, this section will focus on three of the largest: *New Oriental*; *Tomorrow Advancing Life (TAL)*; and *Squirrel AI*. This specific selection offers a particular insight into the ways AI and education have developed over time, from distinct origins in the private education sector. The focus on these particular companies will also continue into the next chapter.

New Oriental is the largest and perhaps the most established private education company in China. Significantly, New Oriental was founded by Yu Minhong in 1993 as an English-language training company, during, as will be discussed below, a particularly intensive time for the proliferation of private education. New Oriental expanded rapidly to become one of the most well-known education companies across China, with Yu Minhong in particular developing something of a celebrity status as an English educator. This renown is demonstrated by a 2013 film which depicts the origins of the company, entitled 'American Dreams in China' (or 中国合伙人 – translated literally as 'Chinese business partners'). The film is significant here in the sense that it depicts the atmosphere and spirit of the time, one of entrepreneurialism fused with wider shifts in Chinese politics and society characterised by the 'opening up' reforms, as will be examined further below. New Oriental was able to exploit these favourable conditions, and in particular the increasing demand for English-language skills, to expand its business into the leading provider of private education in China. Before the recent private education regulations (discussed in detail in the next chapter), New Oriental operated 89 schools and 1,125 learning centres, across which it employed over 30,100 teachers (NOETG 2015a). That the company also owned 18 bookstores (ibid) attests to its substantial operations.

As with many private education companies in China, New Oriental's focus expanded towards preparation for examinations, specifically the Gaokao (高考), or university entrance examination, and the Zhongkao (中考), the high-school entrance examination, as well as the Graduate Record Examinations (GRE) for admission to US graduate schools. The outward orientation of the latter is particularly notable, and reflects the early ethos of New Oriental as a progressive, entrepreneurial company, responding to the shifting needs of a Chinese population increasingly exposed to foreign contexts and ideas (Kleinman et al. 2011). As a company founded in the technology hub of Zhongguancun in northwest Beijing (this area will be examined in detail in Chapter 5), and well-connected in entrepreneurial networks through its charismatic founder Yu Minhong, New Oriental embraced digital technologies as a means of extending its educational offerings. In 2001, the company changed its name to New Oriental Education Technology, and developed various online services, including the 'Koolearn' (新东方在线) platform, offering over 2,000 courses (NOETG 2015a). New Oriental promotes 40.5 million student enrolments across its services (ibid), indicating the substantial sources of data available for the development of AI products. In late 2018, the company announced two projects: 'N-Brain', a strategic network aimed at 'building cooperation among AI-related institutions, investors and businesses', and the 'AI Class Director', a project to develop an elaborate range of data-driven technologies for classroom teaching:

> face and speech recognition, facial attributes analysis, natural language processing and other AI tech to track each student's class performance in real time, analyze their emotions, participation and results in a quantitative approach, giving advice accordingly.
>
> (Qiao Lei quoted in Xu 2018)

However, as will be examined further in the next chapter, despite these high-profile announcements, New Oriental's AI projects appear to have ceased operation, largely as a result of strict government regulations on private education introduced in 2021. Nevertheless, New Oriental has been a substantial part of the development of AI for education in China, acting, as discussed below, as a key funder for a range of education technology start-ups.

Founded in 2003, TAL has also emerged as a significant actor in the development of AI for education. TAL is the English name of the company, updated in 2013, while the Chinese name remains 好未来 (Hao Wei Lai), meaning 'Good Future'. Given that TAL was listed on the New York Stock Exchange in 2010, this name change perhaps reflects a greater interest in international recognition. Indeed, TAL's successes in the private education markets of China allowed the company to invest in well-known US educational businesses Minerva, in 2014, and Knewton, in 2016. As such, TAL is representative of the increasing involvement of Chinese education technology companies in global investor networks. TAL reportedly acquired so-called 'adaptive' AI technology as part of its investment in Knewton (Vinton 2016), which, presumably, it was able to integrate with data derived from its own substantial online educational offerings. TAL advertises a 'diversified educational ecosystem' of sub-brands, platforms and services, including 'Xueersi, Xueersi Online School, Izhikang, First Leap, Tipaipai, Xiaohou AI, Xiaohoucode, Aiqidao, Mamabang, Kaoyanbang, and Shunshunliuxue' (TAL 2017a), demonstrating substantial operations. Through a dedicated 'AI lab', the company describes the application of 'visual, voice, natural language processing and machine learning to assist students in teaching, inspiring students' classroom interest and intelligent interaction' through an 'Intelligent Teaching System', 'Intelligent Practice System', and 'Personalised Learning System' (TAL 2017b).

Significantly, TAL was recently selected by the Chinese Ministry of Science and Technology to represent the area of 'smart education' in the 'National AI team[1]' (see Larsen 2019;) – this will also be discussed further in the next chapter in relation to recent government regulations. This provides TAL with substantial authority as a 'platform' and gatekeeper for the development of AI for education across China, with a remit to support the entrepreneurial development of other small and medium-sized companies, establish business networks, and share data and software (ibid). TAL therefore appears to be enabled to not only acquire and manage public educational data, but also define the future development of the sector. Roberts et al. further contends that:

> Being endorsed as a national champion involves a deal whereby private companies agree to focus on the government's strategic aims. In return, these companies receive preferential contract bidding, easier access to finance, and sometimes market share protection.
>
> (Roberts et al. 2021, p61)

However, rather than simply providing selected companies with specific advantages, Larsen suggests that the 'Champion' system is directed more towards 'enabling structural mechanisms that afford greater participation and innovation in emerging ecosystems and sectors that increasingly will be powered by AI technologies' (2019, p18). To this end, TAL has subsequently developed an 'open platform' for the application of AI to education, which will be examined in the next chapter. TAL also appears to have gained international recognition through such a role, recently signing a three-year deal with UNESCO to promote AI for education[2] (TAL 2019).

The newest of the three companies introduced in this section is YiXue Education (乂学教育) founded in Shanghai in 2014, which offers the platform 'Squirrel AI', a name by which the company now tends to be referred. Both New Oriental and TAL, introduced above, have been investors in the company (see Cheng 2018). Out of all the currently prominent Chinese education companies, Squirrel AI appears to have attracted the most attention in the media, at least outside of China, and is therefore frequently mentioned in reports on the use of AI in education. Indeed, as Hao notes, Squirrel AI is not only one of the largest education companies in China, but it is also 'one of the best-poised to spread overseas' (Hao 2019). The company has promoted its recruitment of overseas expertise, including Tom Mitchell, E. Fredkin University Professor at Carnegie Mellon University, as its Chief AI Officer. Squirrel AI also enlisted Richard Tong, formerly of US company Knewton, and Dan Bindman, one of the developers behind the *Assessment and Learning in Knowledge Spaces* (ALEKS) software, developed at the University of California, Irvine. Within China, Squirrel AI developed considerable renown through a televised 'Human Versus Machine Competition', in which the AI system was pitted against human teachers in a series of contests across China. That the AI was designated the winner is often referenced as evidence of the product's efficacy. In a recent interview, Richard Tong, Chief Architect at Squirrel AI, suggests that the competitions 'were conducted both for publicity and evangelism' (Tong quoted in Goel and Camacho 2020), clearly recognising the promotional value of such a contest.

Squirrel AI has also publicised the establishing of AI research centres with the Chinese Academy of Science, and SRI international, a research institute founded by Stanford University. The company has also reportedly collaborated on AI research with Carnegie Mellon University, the University of California Berkeley, MIT, and Harvard (Hao 2019). As such, Squirrel AI tends to be portrayed as an overtly international education enterprise, despite its business being focused almost exclusively on Chinese private and state education – this will be detailed further in the next chapter. Squirrel AI appears to be a successful education business, not only achieving 'unicorn'[3] status (Hao 2019), but also launching a $1 million prize for AI research in collaboration with the Association for the Advancement of Artificial Intelligence (AAAI).[4] Entitled the *AAAI Squirrel AI Award for Artificial Intelligence for the Benefit of Humanity*, the prize was awarded for the first time in 2020, to Dr Regina Barzilay of the Massachusetts Institute of Technology for research into AI for healthcare (Conner-Simons 2020). This prize is highly significant, in the sense that it seems to shift the company into a role of benevolent leadership within the AI research community, arguably reinforcing its identity as a technology company, rather than an educational provider.

Other notable companies include Yuanfudao, a $15.5 billion start-up backed by Tencent. The company received considerable press attention in 2020 for being valued as the 'world's biggest edtech unicorn' (Ghosh 2020, no page), at the time seeming to focus on online courses rather than AI specifically. However, presumably drawing on data from its '3.7 million paid student users' (ibid), Yuanfudao recently announced the launch of an AI-driven application purported to focus on STEAM (science, technology, engineering, arts, and mathematics) teaching, named 'Pumpkin Science' (Cheng 2021).

VIPKid is another example of a prominent education company that appears to be shifting towards AI. The company's previous focus was connecting Chinese students with teachers, often foreign, using a live video streaming platform. Referring to VIPKid and similar businesses, Lee suggests 'perception AI now allows these platforms to continuously gather data on student engagement through expression and sentiment analysis. That data continually feeds into a student's profile, helping the platforms filter for the kinds of teachers that keep student engaged' (Lee 2018, p123–124).

Notably, this use of AI caused considerable controversy, as teachers accused the company of unfair practices, essentially by using data analysis to develop an AI system that might eventually make teachers redundant (see Meehan vs VIPKid 2021). The company's website now features a lengthy explanation of its use of the technology, suggesting: '[w]hen you hear AI, you might picture robots coming to steal your job. At VIPKid, we believe in using AI to empower teachers, not replace them' (VIPKid 2021). This example highlights some of the tensions and conflicts, here between technological innovation and human labour, that surface through the use of AI, in contrast to the more straightforward visions of vibrant enterprise.

Across these companies, there is a clear relationship between the provision of online education and the subsequent development of AI, as the data gathered and processed from software platforms has been utilised as the basis for the training of machine learning systems. This alludes to another broad imaginary about the value and applicability of AI – that with enough data, AI can be trained towards multiple functions. Within this vision, the companies with access to data become mutable, able to shift their AI expertise towards different sectors. The next section will suggest ways in which China's 'big tech' have increasing seen education as a productive direction for their businesses.

'Big tech' in AI education

Another significant vision for the development of AI for education involves already established 'big tech' companies reorienting their business strategies to undertake educational activity. Often this is portrayed as a benevolent, philanthropical move by businesses, as they seek to turn their profitable AI products towards initiatives with a broader social purpose, in areas that the government has determined to be strategic priorities. In this sense, where China's 'big tech' firms produce educational resources or curricula related to AI, or indeed design-dedicated software platforms or services for schools and after-school markets, such strategies might be understood as attempts to develop aspects of their business that are more 'acceptable' within the prevailing political environment. This has become even more acute in the wake of recent government regulation targeted at the profitable private after-school industry, as will be examined in the next chapter. Furthermore, the production of educational materials related to AI, particularly for schools, bestows a substantial sense of educational authority upon private companies, as they become the authors of standardised knowledge about AI. In this way, China's 'big tech' appears to be moving towards defining a new 'AI curricula' for state education, derived directly from their commercial needs – this will also be examined further in Chapter 6.

One key example is SenseTime (商汤科技, or Shang Tang Keji), a company established in Hong Kong in 2014, primarily around the use of data-driven technologies for computer vision. In just a few years after its launch,

SenseTime was identified as the world's first AI unicorn (Jiang 2018; Shu-Ching 2018) and most valuable AI start-up (Vincent 2018; Marr 2019). Such rapid development, and apparent success, has helped to focus international attention on the development of AI China, and to motivate much in the way of prognostications about the shifting locus of start-up power, once centred on Silicon Valley, but now heading for Beijing (Lee 2018).

SenseTime's success supposedly derives from establishing, through publications within the community of computer vision experts, a leading technical process involving facial recognition algorithms, named 'DeepID', claimed to be superior to Facebook's established technique named 'DeepFace' (see Shu-Ching 2018). With the potential to apply the research in various commercial contexts (the company claims to have clients across the healthcare, financial, retail, security, entertainment, and education sectors[5]), SenseTime began to attract investments, which connected the company to international networks of venture capitalists. A further crucial step involved the company forming partnerships with universities and other private technology companies to support research, as well as becoming involved in national and international organisations aiming at governing technology development. For example, SenseTime partnered with MIT in 2018 as part of a programme to advance AI, and in the same year collaborated with Alibaba to found an AI research lab in Hong Kong. Further, in 2018, SenseTime was named as China's National Open Innovation Platform (as discussed previously in relation to TAL, and sometimes referred to as 'national AI team' or 'national AI champion' – see Larsen 2019;) for image sensing, and became one of the founding members of the Global Artificial Intelligence Academic Alliance (GAIAA), an international network launched by the World Economic Forum to promote the responsible and ethical use of AI globally.

Significantly, SenseTime appears to have become active in education, largely focused on developing educational resources and dedicated AI curriculum. Its website now promotes a dazzling array of educational materials, including textbooks, an 'AI experimental platform' for students and teachers, a broad range of courses on topics such as Human-Computer Interaction and Reinforced Learning, as well as advertised in-person classroom training events, winter and summer schools, and international competitions (see SenseTime 2022). Here, providing education for younger generations to learn the skills associated with AI appears to be promoted as a kind of corporate responsibility, where powerful tech companies devote resources to issues of national importance – in this case, technical training that will support the government's strategic priorities for AI ascendency. Furthermore, this shift to educational provision also seems to entail a substantial degree of control and influence over public sector education. In 2018, SenseTime also launched, to great fanfare in China, a textbook entitled *Fundamentals of Artificial Intelligence*, in collaboration with East China Normal University (SenseTime 2022). As will also be discussed in Chapter 6, the textbook was hailed as the very first of its kind directed towards high-school students (ibid), and was introduced in over 100 Chinese schools across five provinces. This move is highly significant, in the sense that textbooks constitute definitive and authoritative knowledge about AI, particularly where they are established during foundational levels of schooling. In this way, SenseTime appears to have become a powerful educational authority by defining the kinds of subjects and topics deemed most relevant to AI, and heavily influencing the ways young people form an understanding of the associated theories and applications. This private sector influence over China's burgeoning 'AI curriculum' will be examined further in Chapter 6.

Another significant example is the announcement from iFlyTek – a company designated one of China's 'national AI champions' for 'smart audio' – of a 'learning pad' hardware device, loaded with AI software designed to 'diagnose' and 'personalise' educational experiences (iFlyTek 2021). This kind of device, produced for the private after-school market, will also be discussed in the next chapter as a way of specifically avoiding recent regulation. As will also be examined, Squirrel AI has developed a similar product. iFlyTek's shift into this kind of educational product further indicates that education is viewed as a profitable business, as well as a politically acceptable one, as long as AI designs remain on the permissible side of government regulations. Other examples include, as will be examined further in Chapter 6, Baidu recently announcing a collaboration with Beijing Changping Vocational School, to establish a 'vocational school-enterprise cooperation initiative on AI education' (Peterson et al. 2021, p12), suggesting a significant private sector interest in vocational, rather than general, education. The development of educational resources for schools includes *Future Intelligent Creator on AI-Series of Artificial Intelligence Excellent Courses for Primary and Secondary Schools*, produced through a collaboration between East China Normal University and UBTech Robotics, a company backed by Tencent (Peterson et al. 2021). Chapter 6 will also examine the ways companies such as Baidu have partnered with various universities to collaborate on AI research. This is also indicative of a widespread assumption that AI systems and expertise developed for a specific context can be adapted and reapplied to different sectors, in ways that disrupt and revolutionise engrained ways of working.

While the previous sections have conveyed a sense of the productivity, influence, and dynamism of China's AI companies, particularly those focused on education, this vision of a powerful private sector is only partial. In order to develop a deeper understanding, it is necessary to examine the historical contexts through which China's start-up culture, as well as its private education provision, emerged. As will be detailed below, this is a crucial aspect of the Chinese context, due in no uncertain terms to the relative novelty of the private sector in China, as well as its somewhat precarious relationship to the founding ideology of the Chinese Communist Party (CPC). Returning to Lin's (2006) triadic framework of nationalism, socialism, and developmentalism, this section will examine the ways in which the private sector animated the tensions holding this vision of the Chinese state together, and in so doing provide an underlying context through which to better comprehend contemporary discussions of AI and education.

Precarious origins of the private sector

As Lin suggests, business people in China have traditionally been viewed with suspicion and disdain:

> [t]raditionally, the Chinese people have despised businessmen, who ranked below government officials, scholar-intellectuals, and peasants in social status. The commonly held bias is that all businessmen are sleazy and selfish, making money through cheating and ripping off the poor.
>
> (Lin 1999, p19).

Affirming this sense of the perceived inauthenticity and immoral conduct of business people, Jin, writing about ancient China, further describes the precarious lives of business people, rooted in untrustworthiness and insecurity:

> businesspeople belonged to the lower strata of Chinese society … Whenever the government lacked funds, it would fleece business people and property owners, leaving them no space for safety or growth. As a result, wealth was not viewed as an effective means of self-protection. For millennia, the best way to safeguard one's interests in China has been to affiliate oneself with political power.
>
> (Jin 2019, p11)

While such descriptions of traditional culture in China do not justify any kind of grand explanatory theory about the role of business people in Chinese society, they do hint at underlying historical contexts that may differ significantly from those elsewhere, and, at the very least, suggest an already existing set of assumptions that aligned with the much later political orientation of the CPC. Notably, Jin (2019) suggests this view of business people as a fundamental contrast to the US, in which private entrepreneurship and the independent accumulation of wealth often appear to be valorised as core and authentic forms of citizenship, while intervention from a central government is frequently resisted.

It perhaps goes without saying that the establishment of the CPC after 1949 certainly didn't set out to improve the fortune of Chinese business people. From the mid-1950s, under the leadership of Mao Zedong (毛泽东), a state-run, centralised, and planned economy was introduced, where 'private economic activity and the role of the market were severely limited and the role of the state and state-owned enterprises was pervasive'

(Lardy 2014, p11). Thus, the perception of the lowly status of business people was 'further reinforced during Mao's regime, when material motivation was denounced and spiritual reward was glorified by the mass media' (Lin 1999, p19). Indeed, during this period business people were assigned to the broad category of 'class enemies' (Lin 2006, p76). However, despite being almost entirely devoid of an autonomous private sector, this period is important because it established the conditions from which a market economy would eventually (re)surface, in ways that were carefully managed by the government of Deng Xiaoping (邓小平) and his successors. Examining the form of this reintroduction of the private sector is vital to understanding the business of AI development today. The planned economy effectively came to an end in 1978 after the introduction of market-based economic reorganisation, and the so-called 'opening-up' period of reform. Effectively, the category of 'class enemy', which had included business people in Mao's era, was now reinstated as 'working class' and assumed to be reformed (Lin 1999).

Nevertheless, the status of the private sector took some time to become established. As Kleinman et al. suggest, '[b]usiness people ... started from a rather low rank in the early 1980s, when the planned economy dominated and the private sector was regarded as a nondesirable yet necessary complement' (Kleinman et al. 2011, p17). Indeed, it took another decade for the private sector to really become an influential part of Chinese society. However, the 1980s were an important period of apparent liberalism, innovation, and experimentation, through which the private sector evolved and matured; '[w]hat had been anathema in the Maoist era was the acceptance of markets, foreign capital, and entrepreneurialism. All of these were to be tolerated, and then encouraged, as the decade wore on' (Brown 2020, p84). Significantly, then, the 1980s might be seen as an early phase of experimentation with market entrepreneurialism, and as a precursor to the kind of liberal policy strategy discussed in the previous chapter with respect to encouraging the proliferation of technological development. Key sites of reform were in the rural economy as well as through the establishment of Special Economic Zones (or SEZs) (examined further in the Chapter 5), and these developments 'almost doubled' China's per capita and gross GDP measures, from $202 to $341 billion, and from $202 to $390 billion, respectively (Brown 2020, p87). As Brown suggests, 'China still lives, at least economically, in a period brought about by the Dengist reforms' (2020, p87). Nevertheless, it is important not to see this period as one given over entirely to the market. Rather, this decade of reform brought with it significant ideological struggles, as the role of private enterprise increasingly conflicted with socialist values, and a society in which 'Maoism had been a living faith for many Chinese' (Brown 2020, p90). As Lin notes, by the end of the 1980s, traditional views of the business community inverted, and 'judgement of a person's worth, once based on political criteria, now increasingly incline towards wealth and money' (1999, p20). It was from this ideological tussle that the well-rehearsed phrase 'socialism with Chinese characteristics' was derived, specifically from a speech given by Zhao Ziyang at the 1987 Thirteenth Party Congress. The significance of this phrase was in its signalling of the CPC's willingness to adapt socialist principles in ultimately pragmatic ways, to suit the prevailing conditions of the time. Referring again to Lin's (2006) nationalism, socialism, and developmentalism triad, one might suggest this to be a period in which development, driven specifically by private companies as opposed to state-run firms, was not only given priority, but the socialist dimension was also rearticulated in a way that would not expose any ideological rupture. In effect, it was a clear statement that a socialist government would continue at the same time as embracing, and tightly managing, market-based economic reforms. This, therefore, is the foundation of the way the government would continue to operate *with* the private sector, not simply in opposition to it. Building on this foundational period of market reform, the 1990s saw what is generally regarded as a surge in economic expansion, with widely reported measures at the end of the decade indicating an average annual gross GDP of 11.2%, far exceeding the global average of 2.4% over the same period (see People's Daily 2000).

Private education: reform and innovation

As discussed previously, AI development for education in China has been most prominent, not only within the burgeoning tech sector, but also within the domain of private extra-curricular, or after-school, provision. The history of private education in China, therefore, is of equal value in examining the contexts underpinning the contemporary drive for AI-infused education, and offers additional insights about the deep-seated entrepreneurial character of after-school provision today. While the history of private education in China dates back, as Lin (1999) contends, to Confucius himself,[6] it is the market reforms of the late 20th century that offer the greatest insight into the rise of AI and education in contemporary times.

Before 1949, private primary and secondary schools comprised 40% of all schools in the country, offering a wide range of subjects (Lin 1999). By 1947, 79 of the 207 Chinese universities at the time were private institutions of higher education (ibid). However, just like the businesses discussed in the previous section, private education providers were also systematically dismantled under the CPC, and did not re-emerge until the early 1980s, after the 'reform and opening up' policies overseen by Deng Xiaoping, and were focused exclusively on university entrance exam preparation (Lin 1999). Here we see the foundation of the contemporary private education sector in China, which has maintained this core focus on training for examinations. Nevertheless, private provision quickly expanded, and by the mid-1980s was offering a range of additional credentials and skills development (Lin 1999). This expansion was formalised through two key policies: 'The Decision of the Communist Party of China on the Reform of China's

Education Structure' in 1985, and the Education Act of 1986, both of which made explicit strategic directives to promote the establishment of private schools (Wang 2001).

Significantly, 1992 saw huge growth in the private education sector, and, as Lin (1999) describes, this expansion was linked explicitly to Deng Xiaoping's famous visit to the south of China, which was symbolic of the leadership's continued commitment to market reforms (Brown 2020). Indeed, the intensification of economic growth instigated by Deng's tour fuelled a vast expansion of the private education sector throughout the 1990s. As Kleinman et al. note, 'the marketization of education' (2011, p15) was one of three major reforms undertaken by the state in this period.[7] Further, as Wang (2001) and Sun (2010) suggest, the bourgeoning of private provision also resulted from the inability of the strained public education sector to provide the kind of educational reforms needed to drive wider economic transformation. Private education was thus tolerated and encouraged as an important source of expertise that could contribute to national development goals. There is an important parallel to be drawn here with the contemporary private education sector, including after-school training, which might therefore be understood, not simply in commercial terms, but as an important and accepted part of educational provision more broadly.

Private education was also intertwined with social changes that were instigated by the 1978 reforms, as Chinese society diversified, and thus came to perceive education as able to offer different kinds of opportunities. As Kleinman et al. (2011) describe, the post-1978 reform period was one in which the social structure of China underwent profound transformations, away from the communal structures established in the Mao era, and towards a growing sense of individualism, as well as high social mobility. Rapid urbanisation (also examined in Chapter 5) and social stratification led directly to the demand for more diverse educational offerings, which the state sector was too often unable to supply (Lin 1999). As Lin (1999) further suggests, English-language education was one of the subjects in high demand, and it was in response to this new market that New Oriental became established, as outlined above. Private schools 'sprang up throughout the country, especially during the period of 1992–1995, when the country's economic development was heated up to an unprecedented degree' (Lin 1999, p6). Lin notes how one particular private school named Guangya Primary School, established in Chengdu in the Western Sichuan province, achieved widespread attention, in particular for its technological advances, such as 'computers, color TVs, and pianos installed in air-conditioned classrooms' (1999, p6). It is important to also emphasise the economic fervour of the time, summed up by Lin as 'a mentality that one is not only to become rich but to become rich in a very fast and easy way…[i]t is in this context that private schools, using Chairman Mao's famous saying, have spread from "sparkles" into "a prairie of fire"' (1999, p20). Importantly, Lin notes how the rise of private education was focused predominantly in cities, where urbanities 'longed to learn new skills in order to seize opportunities in the new market economy' (1999, p7). This particular focus in cities is examined further in Chapter 5.

Particularly noteworthy in this period are the conditions and strategies through which companies sought to capitalise on the economic conditions of the time, and create and exploit the formation of new educational markets. Lin suggests, '[c]onnecting themselves with the needs of the market, the schools operated in a highly efficient manner' (1999, p7), indicating a capacity to function in ways unhindered by the slow-moving bureaucratic structures of the public sector, perceived as unable to adapt to changing conditions in society. Wang (2001) emphasises the 'market' analogy in suggesting that private schools were explicitly modelled as 'providers' for parents as 'consumers', and were 'geared to parents' wishes', for example, through the offering of 'enhanced English and computer courses' (Wang 2001, p107). Further describing the methods and approaches adopted by the new private education companies of the 1990s, Lin captures the sense of entrepreneurialism, invention, and excitement of the time:

> They simply splashed their ads across the streets of the city or set up a booth at a heavy intersection announcing their programs. Adopting a 'guerrilla' strategy, they offered whatever was in hot demand...The duration of their programs could be short or long, and classes could be taken during the day or night, all depending on the needs of the clientele. To attract enrollment, they even promised to refund fees if the students were not satisfied.
>
> (Lin 1999, p7)

Here we see the sense of spontaneity, enterprise, and innovation that, arguably, continues in private after-school education today, at least until the recent 'double reduction' regulations (examined in the next chapter). As such, within this after-school market, AI might be understood as merely the latest in an array of techniques and practices adopted to develop and exploit shifting educational markets and consumer demands. However, the eagerness for private provision in the 1990s was not always matched with educational experience and know-how, with some ventures being initiated 'without much expertise, and with only enthusiasm and a sense of adventure' (Wang 2001, p113). Regulation thus developed into a significant concern. Private provision also surfaced concerns about inequality (Wang 2001), particularly where 'elite' schools emerged to exclusively serve 'rich private business entrepreneurs', foreigners, and 'some government officials' (Lin 1999, p12). Nevertheless, the broader impact of these controversies was, importantly, the encouragement of public debate about the purpose of education and how it should be governed (Wang 2001). In this sense, alongside the development of markets and the growing of educational businesses, privatisation was clearly linked to notions of educational reform and progress (Tiehua 1996; Lin 1999; Wang 2001). As Wang notes, 'private institutions seem to offer a fresh burst of energy to the Chinese education system' (Wang 2001, p105). Further, many of the new private education entrepreneurs expressed a desire 'to experiment with new educational philosophies that would be impossible in the public school system' (Wang 2001, p108). It is important to see this belief in innovation, and in a sense of breaking free of the constraints of the traditional public educational structure, as foundational to the outlook of the private education sector, and a legacy that has continued into contemporary experimentations with AI. However, despite the potential for educational innovation, it is vital to note that private provision was still ultimately evaluated according to the performance of pupils in the Gaokao (高考), as well as in preparatory testing for examinations (Lin 1999). In this sense, the formal standardising practices of the state still had a significant role in defining the character of private provision.

Concluding remarks

This chapter examined the role of the private sector in developing relationships between AI and education, and nurturing a distinctive imaginary about the promise of data-driven educational activity. AlphaGo's defeat of well-known Go players provided a compelling narrative for the private sector in China, subsequently developing a vision of creative entrepreneurial activity driving the country's AI development. It is into this vision that various projections of educational AI have emerged, frequently portraying China as a vast source of unregulated data, rapid technical development, and huge populations of willing student-consumers.

Three key companies have emerged around the development of AI, all deriving from the private after-school sector: New Oriental, with origins in English education during the early 1990s; TAL, having developed substantial international networks, and offering a wide range of products and sub-brands; and Squirrel AI, developing a highly publicised 'personalised' learning platform, and targeting after-school markets in second- and third-tier cities. Aside from dedicated education companies, China's 'big tech' firms, such as SenseTime, are also increasingly shifting into different forms of educational provision, developing a range of textbooks, curricula, and learning materials for AI, often directed at the school level.

Offering some context for this commercial activity, the chapter also outlined a history of the private sector in China, as well as a history of private educational provision, focusing on the after-school sector from which the above companies derived. This section suggested themes of both precarity and enterprise, conveying the dual sense of instability and enthusiasm that characterises entrepreneurial endeavours in the tech sector in China, and those particularly concerned with developing AI for education. Such perspectives appear to be substantially overlooked in the wider imaginaries of China's proliferating 'ed tech' communities, which tend to portray zealous entrepreneurial activity, often as an incentive for investment.

Notes

1 The 'National AI Champions' was launched in late 2017 with just four nomi-nated private companies (Baidu, Alibaba, Tencent, and SenseTime). In 2019, the 'champions' were expanded to 19, at which point a category of 'smart education' was established, and TAL nominated for the role.
2 Also see UNESCO's project page for updates and reports about the collabora-tion: https://en.unesco.org/themes/ict-education/ai-futures-learning
3 'Unicorn' here refers to a term coined by venture capital investor Aileen Lee in 2013, in order to designate a start-up company valued at over $1 billion. The term was chosen to indicate the rarity of such a valuation.
4 See https://aaai.org/Organization/organization.php
5 See https://www.sensetime.com/me-en
6 This would be 551–479 BCE, corresponding with the final stages of the spring and autumn period of ancient China, 771 to 476 BCE.
7 The other two major reforms of the 1990s were the privatisation of housing and the marketisation of medical care.

References

Beard, A. (2020). Can computers ever replace the classroom? *The Guardian*. 19 March. https://www.theguardian.com/technology/2020/mar/19/can-computers-ever-replace-the-classroom

Bory, P. (2019). Deep new: The shifting narratives of artificial intelligence from Deep Blue to AlphaGo. *Convergence*, *25*(4), 627–642. https://doi.org/10.1177/1354856519829679

Bray, C. (2014). "Google Acquires British Artificial Intelligence Developer". Deal-Book. *The New York Times*. 27 January. https://archive.nytimes.com/dealbook.nytimes.com/2014/01/27/google-acquires-british-artificial-intelligence-developer/

Brown, K. (2020). *China*. Cambridge: Polity Press

Cheng, Y. (2018). Adaptive learning boosted by AI tech. *China Daily*. Accessed 20 May 2019. http://www.chinadaily.com.cn/a/201804/12/WS5acee9efa3105cdcf6517da5.html

Cheng, Y. (2021). Yuanfudao launches AI-powered science education product. *China Daily*. 30 July. https://www.chinadaily.com.cn/a/202107/30/WS6103a021a310efa1bd6658d6.html

Chu, B. (2013). Chinese whispers: Why everything you've heard about China is wrong. London: Weidenfeld & Nicolson.

Conner-Simons, A. (2020). Regina Barzilay wins $1M association for the advancement of artificial intelligence squirrel AI award. *MIT News*. 23 September. https://news.mit.edu/2020/regina-barzilay-wins-aaai-squirrel-ai-award-artificial-intelligence-0923

Deloitte. (2019). Global artificial intelligence industry whitepaper. *Deloitte*. 1 June. https://www2.deloitte.com/cn/en/pages/technology-media-and-telecommunications/articles/global-ai-development-white-paper.html

Ghosh, M. (2020). Yuanfudao becomes world's biggest Edtech Unicorn with US$2.2B funding. *Jumpstart*. 23 October. https://www.jumpstartmag.com/yuanfudao-becomes-worlds-biggest-edtech-unicorn/

Goel, A., & Camacho, I. (2020). Squirrel AI award for artificial intelligence for the benefit of humanity - An interview with Squirrel AI's Richard Tong. *Interactive AI Magazine*. 28 May. https://interactiveaimag.org/columns/articles/interview/squirrel-ai-award-for-artificial-intelligence-to-benefit-humanity/

Guo, S. (2021). *The evolution of the Chinese internet: Creative visibility in the digital public*. Stanford: Stanford University Press.

Hao, K. (2019). China has started a grand experiment in AI education. It could reshape how the world learns. *MIT Technology Review*. Accessed 16 September 2019. https://www.technologyreview.com/2019/08/02/131198/china-squirrel-has-started-a-grand-experiment-in-ai-education-it-could-reshape-how-the/

iFlyTek. (2021). iFLYTEK releases new IFLYTEK learning pad. 24 August. http://www.iflytek.com/en/news/193.html

Jiang, S. (2018). China's SenseTime raises $620 million, its second funding round in two months. *Reuters*. 31 May. Available: https://www.reuters.com/article/us-sensetime-funding/chinas-sensetime-raises-620-million-its-second-funding-round-in-two-months-idUSKCN1IW07I

Jin, H. (2019). *The Banished Immortal: A life of Li Bai*. New York: Pantheon Books.

Kleinman, A., Yan, Y., Jun, J, Lee, S., Zhang, E., Tianshu, P., Fei, W., and Jinhua, G. (2011). *Deep China: the moral life of the person*. Berkley: The University of California Press.

Lardy, N. (2014). *Markets Over Mao: The Rise of Private Business in China*. Washington: Peterson Institute for International Economics

Larsen, B.C. (2019). China's national AI team: The role of National AI open innovation platforms. In *AI Policy and China: Realities of State-Led Development*, G. Webster (Ed.). Stanford-New America Digichina Project Special Report No. 1. pp. 21–25. https://newamerica.org/documents/4353/DigiChina-AI-report-20191029.pdf

Lee, K-F. (2018). *AI superpowers: China, silicon valley, and the new world order*. New York: Houghton Mifflin Harcourt.

Lee, K.-F. (2021). China's Ed tech unicorns prove that remote learning can work. *Wired*. 5 February. https://www.wired.co.uk/article/kai-fu-lee-china-ed-tech

Lin, J. (1999). *Social transformation and private education in China*. Westport, CT: Praeger

Lin, C. (2006). *The transformation of Chinese socialism*. Durham, NC: Duke University Press.

Marr, B. (2019). Meet the world's most valuable AI startup: China's SenseTime. *Forbes*. 17 June 2019. Available: https://www.forbes.com/sites/bernardmarr/2019/06/17/meet-the-worlds-most-valuable-ai-startup-chinas-sensetime/?sh=3a81ab04309f

Meehan v. Vipkid. (2021). CV 20–6370 (JS) (AKT) (E.D.N.Y. Aug. 27, 2021) https://casetext.com/case/meehan-v-vipkid-1

Ni, D. 2021. China's Tutoring Ban Leaves a Trail of Debt, Anger, and Broken Dreams. *Sixth Tone*. 1st November *https://www.sixthtone.com/news/1008838*

NOETG (New Oriental Education and Technology Group). (2015a). Overview. Accessed 2 June 2019. http://www.neworiental.org/english/who/201507/8213540.html

People's Daily. (2000). *China's average economic growth in 90s ranked 1st in world*. http://en.people.cn/english/200003/01/eng20000301X115.html

Peterson, D., Goode, K., & Gehlhaus, D. (2021). AI Education in China and the United States: A comparative assessment. CSET [Center for Security and Emerging Technology] Issue Brief. September 2021. Available: https://cset.georgetown.edu/wp-content/uploads/CSET-AI-Education-in-China-and-the-United-States-1.pdf

Qi, J. (2020). 8 Chinese EdTech start-ups leading the global educational technology industry. *Daxue Consulting*. 23 June. https://daxueconsulting.com/china-edtech-educational-technology-market/

Roberts, H., Cowls, J., Morley, J., Taddeo, M., Wang, V., & Floridi, L. (2021). The Chinese approach to artificial intelligence: an analysis of policy, ethics, and regulation. *AI & Society*, 36, 59–77. https://doi.org/10.1007/s00146-020-00992-2

Sensetime. (2022). *Primary AI education.* https://www.sensetime.com/en/product-education-01?categoryId=1169

Shu-Ching, J.C. (2018). The faces behind China's artificial intelligence unicorn. *Forbes*. Accessed 29 September 2019. https://www.forbes.com/sites/shuchingjeanchen/2018/03/07/the-faces-behind-chinas-omniscient-video-surveillance-technology/#2089de664afc

Sun, M. (2010). Education system reform in China after 1978: Some practical implications. *International Journal of Educational Management*, 24(4), 314–329. DOI: 10.1108/09513541011045254

TAL [Tomorrow Advancing Life]. (2017a). About TAL. https://en.100tal.com/who

TAL [Tomorrow Enhancing Life]. (2017b). Educational technology. https://www.100tal.com/technology/

TAL [Tomorrow Enhancing Life]. (2019). TAL Joins Hands with UNESCO to Promote Educational Development. *Cision PR Newswire*. 15 April. https://www.prnewswire.com/news-releases/tal-joins-hands-with-unesco-to-promote-educational-development-300831871.html

Tiehua, Q. (1996). A brief description of current private school development in china. *Chinese Education & Society*, 29(2), 31–40. DOI: 10.2753/CED1061–1932290231

Tracxn. (2022). AI in education startups in China. *Tracxn*. 28 March. https://tracxn.com/explore/AI-in-Education-Startups-in-China

Vincent, J. (2018). The world's most valuable AI startup is a Chinese company specializing in real-time surveillance. *The Verge*. Accessed 3 September 2019. https://www.theverge.com/2018/4/11/17223504/ai-startup-sensetime-china-most-valuable-facial-recognition-surveillance

Vinton, K. (2016). This Former PhD Student From China Turned A Tutoring Chain Into A Billion Dollar Fortune. *Forbes*. Accessed 4 September 2019. https://www.forbes.com/sites/katevinton/2016/04/14/this-former-phd-student-from-china-turned-a-tutoring-chain-into-a-billion-dollar-fortune/#70b4cfa12ff9

VIPKid. (2021). How using AI in education empowers teachers. *VIPKidblog*. 23 March. https://blog.vipkid.com/how-can-artificial-intelligence-help-teachers-vipkid-blog/

Wang, P. (2001). Private education emerges in modern China: A comparative case study. *NUCB Journal of Language Culture and Communication*, 3(2), 105–115.

Xi, J. (2017). Secure a decisive victory in building a moderately prosperous society in all respects and strive for the great success of socialism with Chinese characteristics for a new era. Delivered at the 19th national congress of the communist party of China, 18 Oct 2017.

Xu, W. (2018, October 31). China's New Oriental Unveils AI-Related Education Initiatives. YiCai Global. https://www.yicaiglobal.com/news/china-new-oriental-unveils-ai-related-educationinitiatives

Yu, K. (2019). Private education. *Chinese Education & Society*, 52(1–2), 1–2. https://doi.org/10.1080/10611932.2019.1606605

Zhao, G. (2016). China's historical encounter with the West and Modern Chinese education. In G. Zhao & Z. Deng (Eds.) *Re-envisioning Chinese education: The meaning of person-making in a new age*. Abingdon: Routledge. pp. 13–33.

4 'Double reduction' and the return of the state

Rather than beginning with the outline of a particular sociotechnical imaginary of artificial intelligence (AI), as in other chapters, this chapter continues from the examination of policy in Chapter 2. Thus, the subsequent discussion is grounded in the policy-driven imaginary outlined previously, one that not only derives from technical assumptions about AI's capacity to induce straightforward economic transformations, but is also inflected by notions of data-driven geopolitical rivalry. However, perhaps most important here is the vision that AI technologies can be controlled and managed by the state, and tuned to the shifting needs of national development. This was one of the central themes discussed in Chapter 2, where a cluster of recent policies related to AI was suggested to shape the wider sociotechnical imaginary by re-establishing centralised governance as the driving force for future visions of data-driven transformation.

Building on this combined vision, this chapter analyses a recent set of regulations that, while not directly linked to AI, dramatically and abruptly impacted the education landscape, and the direction of data-driven technology development. While the previous two chapters have outlined the broad relationships between the state and the private sector in relation to AI for education, comprising imaginaries of centralised policy incentivisation (Chapter 2) and visions of a fertile entrepreneurial culture around tech development (Chapter 3), this chapter offers an example of a direct collision between the two. This doesn't mean that the state and the private sector were necessarily operating in opposition where AI and education were concerned, but the specific policy initiative examined below certainly signals a willingness on the part of the government to seek to manage and control (private) education, with the subsequent effect of pulling technical expertise closer to the public domain. As will be examined below, while the policy in question wasn't directed at AI specifically, one of the key consequences of the regulation, so this chapter argues, has been, not only to curb the ability of the private sector to develop and deploy such technology in education, but also to nudge and entice key commercial organisations into greater affiliations with the state. However, as will be detailed below, the regulations have also ended up pushing AI development for education into new areas,

DOI: 10.4324/9781003375135-4

as the private sector has sought to find other outlets for their entrepreneurial impulses. Examining this mutable terrain, this chapter further expands upon the shifting relationships between government and entrepreneurship in the development of AI for education, and the conflicting imaginaries of state control and commercial innovation.

The 'double reduction'

On the 24 July 2021, the Ministry of Education published a new policy detailing a number of restrictions on private education companies in China (see MEPRC 2021). Officially entitled 'Opinions on Further Reducing the Work Burden of Students in Compulsory Education and the Burden of Off-campus Training' (关于进一步减轻义务教育阶段学生作业负担和校外培训负担的意见), the policy tended to be referred to as the 'double reduction' (双减, or 'shuang jiao'), indicating the multi-layered and severe restrictions on the private education sector. The central feature of the policy was the prohibition of capital operations in the private education sector, and the requirement that all businesses in this area re-register as non-profit organisations. In other words, the private education sector – by some estimates worth $100 billion (Bloomberg 2021a), by others $300 billion (Ni 2021a), at least before the *double reduction* policy – was no longer able to turn a profit. As such, the *double reduction* was widely interpreted as decimating the private education industry in China (e.g. Che 2021; Ma 2021), and drastically reducing the stock value of key companies (see E. Cheng 2021). While this economic fallout seemed to be the primary focus of reporting about the *double reduction* outside of China, presumably due to the large private education companies being understood primarily as investment opportunities (as discussed in the previous chapter), the policy included a broad set of regulations, seeming to be directed more towards the management of the sector than its demise. This included barring 'monopolies', constraining advertising, and compelling companies to standardise and publicise pricing (MEPRC 2021). Further conditions appeared oriented towards a genuine concern for the highly competitive and pressurised education system in China – conditions which the private industry is often accused of intensifying (Xue 2021) – through the prohibition of private tuition during evenings, weekends, and holidays (MEPRC 2021). Indeed, the 'reduction of work burden for students' included in the full title of the policy signals what is intended to be a core feature of the regulation, but one that has been overlooked by the shortened *double reduction*. In this way, the policy might be understood, at least in part, as a reaction to long-standing concerns over the pressures placed on Chinese students, perhaps most acutely through the somewhat infamous university entrance exam, or Gaokao (高考), but also the lesser acknowledged senior high school entrance exam, or Zhongkao (中考) (discussed further in Chapter 7). Partly due to the anxiety caused by these tests, Xue suggests that '[t]he average amount spent on extracurricular tutoring per student doubled between 2016 and 2018, to nearly 5,000 yuan' (2021). Xue further terms the private sector a 'shadow education' in China that 'exacerbates the problems of the country's test-oriented education system' and has been evolving as 'a key mechanism for maintaining and reinforcing social classes' (2021). In a depiction redolent of the early years of the private education industry in China as examined in the previous chapter, advertising from contemporary 'ed tech' companies has been described as appearing:

> everywhere from subway stations to elevators and online, ranging from benign promos to aggressive ads that suggest their children would be stuck in blue-collar jobs if they don't act now. In 2021's first half, education and tutoring ads accounted for about 9% of the total number of ads displayed on Tencent's and Baidu Inc.'s online platforms.
>
> (Bloomberg News 2021)

As such, it is perhaps no surprise that an official survey by the Ministry of Education reported overwhelming parental support for the policy (see Chen 2021). However, the fallout from the *double reduction* has not been quite the clean-up sometimes implied. Reporting at the time, Ni suggested that 'the industry is undergoing a messy and painful collapse – with ordinary families and workers the collateral damage' (2021). Many parents lost money as private education companies collapsed, while other businesses struggled to maintain employees through the switch to non-profit status (see Ni 2021a). This prompted authorities in Beijing to offer 10,300 jobs, 'including teaching, management, and marketing roles, among others' (Du 2021) to those impacted by the policy. Further, as Ni (2021b) reports, parental anxiety has often been amplified by the *double reduction* restrictions, which may effectively manage commercial activity in the sector, but do not necessarily remove the wider social pressures around children's education in China.

Aside from the charged atmosphere that has developed around the *double reduction* policy, less attention has been given to the indirect, yet nevertheless significant, impact on AI development for education. As discussed in detail in the previous chapter, the substantial private education sector in China has been a key part of the development of the technology for education. While the vast majority of the sector involved in-person teaching, a significant facet had developed through the use of online platforms, in particular for exam preparation, as well as the teaching of foreign languages such as English, where online technologies could connect students to native speakers abroad, but also develop newer markets in less-developed areas of China. In general, however, it is important to note that 'online' forms of private tuition in China tended to be regarded as inferior to more traditional forms of 'in-person' classes', particularly so in the more developed eastern cities and by the wealthy middle class. Nevertheless, the use of technology became established, with key companies such as New Oriental and

Tomorrow Advancing Life (TAL) (introduced in the previous chapter) developing sizeable online aspects to their businesses, from which huge volumes of data could be gathered for the training of AI systems. As has been the narrative depicted about the rise of AI technologies elsewhere (e.g. Alpaydin 2016), these online platforms were able to produce considerable amounts of data about the learning behaviours of such student populations. With the advent of machine learning techniques, such databases were imbued with considerable value, and perceived as prized sources for the production of AI technologies to support the various agendas of the private education sector. Thus, while the *double reduction* policy was designed to target non-state educational activity broadly, and as will be discussed further below, intended to rein in a powerful sector with considerable influence over the learning pathways and study experiences of Chinese youth, it also impacts the organisations that are at the forefront of developing and deploying AI technologies in educational settings. Another key example here is Squirrel AI (also introduced in the previous chapter), a company focused specifically on lower socio-economic populations in second- and third-tier cities, where the technology is marketed as substituting for a lack of quality teachers. This is another sense in which AI has been at the fringes of the *double reduction* regulations, but nonetheless in a position where the policy has had a substantial impact on its trajectory. Indeed, as the subsequent sections will explore in detail, these three companies – New Oriental, TAL, and Squirrel AI – offer important examples of the ways the policy has shaped AI development indirectly through the attempts to manage private after-school training.

The 'double reduction' impact on AI

Although it is important to view the *double reduction* policy in broad terms, and primarily as an attempt to regulate a private education industry that operates largely in the form of face-to-face classroom tuition, the impact on AI, although less direct, is also significant. The full repercussions of the policy may take some time to ripen and settle; however, a number of discernible outcomes are worth outlining here, for the purposes of examining how the *double reduction* has altered the education landscape, and shifted the trajectories of AI development. The following sections will describe the impact of the policy, in turn, on three key private education companies in China, those also discussed in detail in the previous chapter: New Oriental; TAL; and Squirrel AI. The *double reduction* appears to have shaped the direction of these companies considerably, although, as will be described below, very differently, and it is across this difference that a shift in the direction of AI development is apparent. This shift is, unmistakably, a drawing of AI innovation, away from the unregulated domains of private education, and towards the state. Crucially, therefore, the influence of the *double reduction* policy offers an example of the ways the policy-induced imaginaries of government-controlled AI begin to materialise in on-the-ground shifts in the design and deployment of the technology. While the policy was primarily a move to curb the power and influence of the private education sector, and alleviate some of the intense pressure and competition around extra-curricular study, it also had the result, whether directly intentional or not, of regulating AI. The three accounts below each provide a different perspective on this regulation.

New Oriental and the shift to agricultural produce

As suggested in the previous chapter, as one of the most established private education companies in China, New Oriental embodies a particular sense of entrepreneurialism and outward-facing internationalism, given its origins in the fervent markets of English-language training in the early 1990s. In many ways, New Oriental's response to the *double reduction* typified this particular orientation, seeming to return to its industrious roots as educational marketeers.

As with many other private education companies, New Oriental was reported as experiencing an immense fall in share value in the immediate period after the announcement of the regulation, by some measures dropping 54.2% (Cheng 2021). Other reports detail substantial job losses and drastic salary cuts (see Lui 2021; Ni 2021a). Their apparent response to this otherwise devastating loss of value, combined with the prospect of ceasing all capital operations from private educational activity enforced by the *double reduction*, was to dramatically shift the focus of the business. As was reported widely in Chinese media at the time – with this reporting being a testament to New Oriental's prominence in the private education sector – the company announced in November 2021 that it was to relaunch itself as 'an online marketplace for agriculture products' (Wu 2021) in order to account for losses resulting from the regulation. Furthermore, the well-known and charismatic founder and CEO of the company, Yu Minhong, publicised that he would be personally joining other New Oriental teachers in hosting livestreamed sessions to sell a range of farm produce. Indeed, rather than necessarily finding themselves out of their comfort zone, or indeed employment, New Oriental teachers were suggested to have unique sets of skills for the online sales industry, with one private school founder commenting that '[they] are born influencers, and livestreaming is a perfect way to transform their pedagogical skills into sales skills' (Yang Zhi quoted in Wu 2021). By the spring of 2022, New Oriental's shift seemed to have become a success, through a somewhat bizarre, but clearly effective, combination of English and Chinese language in livestream commerce (Zhang 2022). As was reported extensively (e.g. Cao 2022; Zhang 2022), early streams from the company's new enterprise appeared to attract significant attention online, ostensibly due to supplementing online sales with English terms and dialogue more commonly found in language learning scenarios. Cao reports a 'gross merchandise volume (GMV)' from one of these sessions as totalling more than ¥15 million (2022).

What might on the surface appear to be a rather strange turn of events for one of the best-known education companies in China, the shift to livestream sales of agricultural produce reveals, not only something fundamental about the entrepreneurial workings of the private education market, but also some valuable insights about the precarity of AI development. Rather than necessarily constituting a radical shift for New Oriental, the rearticulation of commercial direction might be seen as more of a continuity, as the company strove to maintain its business in the new regulatory landscape. Indeed, the rapid modification of the enterprise to capitalise on the shifting market seemed akin to the 'guerrilla' entrepreneurialism of the early boom in private education (as discussed in the previous chapter). As one report suggested of the recent livestream sales successes, the '[t]eachers seem to have changed careers, but they don't seem to change; New Oriental seems to have changed, but it doesn't seem to have changed' (Li 2022). In other words, the market and the product might have shifted, but the spirit of capitalising on the opportunity has remained the same. While in one sense New Oriental appeared to maintain their entrepreneurial origins, it is also worth noting the particular choice of direction for the company. Selling agricultural products is a 'safe' direction of travel politically, given that it ostensibly supports rural food producers (as appears to be the case in the prominent examples mentioned above), and therefore an agenda of national development. In this sense, e-commerce for agricultural products is the opposite of English-language tuition, an internal orientation as opposed to an outward-facing one.

While New Oriental's shift in commercial direction might be read as a return to its entrepreneurial origins (one interpretation portrays Yu Minhong as returning to his 'rural roots', given the agricultural settings from which the farm produce will be sold – see Li 2021), one might also infer important insights for the development of AI for education. The grand projects announced in 2018 – the 'N-Brain' and 'AI Class Director' (introduced in the previous chapter) – now, perhaps unsurprisingly, receive no mention, suggesting that New Oriental may have ended up a minor player in the development of AI as a result of the *double reduction*. However, education doesn't quite seem to have left the agenda, with Yu Minhong being quoted as suggesting that profits from the recent e-commerce success would be channelled into 'selling educational products such as books, software, hardware, and other cultural and educational supplies' (Cao 2022). As suggested above, non-curriculum subjects and vocational training do not fall under the restrictions imposed by the *double reduction*, and therefore may be seen as potential areas for New Oriental to continue its commercial educational endeavours. While in one sense New Oriental's direction seems to get more confusing as the impact of the regulation takes hold, the constant factor appears to be the market, and the company's evident willingness, if not enthusiasm, for commercial activity. What one might glean from this example, then, is the somewhat fragile state of affairs from which private sector educational AI development emerges, and the clear imperative for a viable business to drive the process. Without an ability to generate profits, there is no loyalty to the ideals of AI development. By the very same virtue, the commitment to education itself becomes just as fickle, and perhaps, soon to be side-lined for a more profitable venture. In the case of New Oriental, however, it would seem unwise to make any predictions about their extraordinary capacity to capitalise on the moment.

TAL and the Open AI Platform

While New Oriental seems to have remained authentic to its entrepreneurial roots, TAL appears to have taken an opposing route, by shifting towards a semi-state role. As mentioned in the previous chapter, TAL was awarded such a position in the form of a 'national AI champion' for smart education in 2019 (Larsen 2019; Wernberg-Tougaard 2021), supposedly placing it in a powerful position of authority over the development of educational AI nationally.

Just like New Oriental, TAL's share value dropped dramatically following the announcement of the *double reduction*, reported as a 70.8% fall (E. Cheng 2021). Significant job losses were also predicted (Liu 2021). While some reports suggested that the company was continuing with non-curriculum subjects (e.g. De Silva 2021) as a way of avoiding the regulation, others suggested a similarity with the 希望学 (Xi Wang Xue) platform, translated as 'Hope Online School', or 'Hope Study', which itself was marketed as 'operating in strict compliance with national policies and regulations' (Xi Wang Xue 2022). It remains unclear whether there is a formal connection between TAL and Xi Wang Xue. However, the company released a statement in late 2021, confirming that it would cease operations conflicting with the *double reduction* regulations, further adding:

> By leveraging its leading-edge education technology, high quality content and extensive experience, TAL will continue to operate and develop the portion of its business that is not related to K9 Academic AST [after school training] Services, and will also explore other opportunities to provide education services in accordance with relevant rules and regulations.
>
> (TAL Education Group 2021a)

At the time of writing, it is therefore uncertain how the commercial aspects of the business will continue. However, notably, TAL's position as an 'AI Champion' appears to be continuing to mature. As a host of promotional material on their 'Artificial Intelligence Open Innovation Platform[1]' website makes clear, TAL now ostensibly provides open access to a range of AI technologies and services, under broad categories of education optical character recognition (OCR), smart correction, face analysis, human analysis, image video analysis, speech recognition, speech synthesis, and voice evaluation (TAL 2021a). Such services are advertised as freely available, upon registration, to other education companies looking to add AI functionalities to their existing educational applications. The specific services seem vast, from more conventional applications of AI, such as mathematical formula recognition or real-time speech recognition, to more unusual examples, such as the 'face search' application for automatic attendance registration, or the 'dress detection' service, described as able to 'intelligently identify teachers' clothing exposure problems in videos and pictures' (TAL 2021b).

The extent to which these AI services and applications are being taken up by education start-ups in China is not clear. However, underpinning TAL's suite of offerings is clearly a productive AI research and development laboratory, and one that, at least on the surface, appears to be focused on open access rather than any explicit commercial activity. Further, there are indications that the AI systems being developed are highly capable. A range of competition awards are promoted on their website (TAL 2021c), including many from prestigious international computer science conferences, such as NeurIPS (the Conference and Workshop on Neural Information Processing Systems), UbiComp, and CVPR (the conference on Computer Vision and Patter Recognition).

One notable example here is a group from TAL winning the 'EmotioNet Challenge' in 2020 (see EmotioNet 2019), a competition devised as part of a workshop entitled 'Challenges and Promises of Inferring Emotion from Images and Video' at the CVPR conference in the same year. TAL's own announcement about the award described the challenge as 'one of the most revered academic competitions in the field of human facial expression recognition' (TAL Education Group 2021b). Indeed, as described and defined by the organisers,[2] the challenge appears to be rather complex, involving significant inferences about the relationships between facial expressions and emotional states:

> faces offer information that helps us navigate our social world, influence whom we love, and determine who we trust or who we believe to be guilty of a crime. But to what extent does an individual's face reveal the person's internal emotions? To what extent (and how) can we design computer vision systems to accurately interpret an emotion or intention from a raised eyebrow, a curled lip, or a narrowed eye?
>
> (EmotioNet 2019)

Aside from the complexities of the 'multi-task learning' techniques deployed by the TAL team to address the image recognition challenge (see Wang et al. 2020), the competition is revealing about the direction of AI development for education in China in a number of ways. First, as the above description makes clear, linking 'correct' emotional states to particular facial expressions is not an explicit educational dilemma, but is rather presented as a purely technical challenge, in which image recognition systems are compared to human interpretive abilities. That an organisation focused on education has demonstrated leading techniques in this area suggests an underlying assumption about the development of AI in general: that particular approaches tend to be developed as purely technical processes, and only subsequently applied to specific contexts, in this example, education. In other words, a demand for the automated emotional recognition of facial expressions did not derive from the education sector itself, but is rather an interest that has originated in computer science disciplines, and is being subsequently inferred as a useful application within educational activity, presumably to identify student responses to specific educational content. Furthermore, the advanced state of Wang et al.'s (2020) research appears to demonstrate a willingness at TAL to push forward the application of such techniques in education. TAL's own announcement about the competition result was explicit about where the research would end up: '[c]urrently, this technology is also made available to the entire education industry through TAL's Open AI Platform' (TAL Education Group 2021b).

Rather than commercialising what is clearly an internationally recognised technique, TAL appear to be embracing its role as a platform for the advancement of AI in education, where research and development seems to lead directly to the deployment of open access tools and services for the broader education technology sector. Elsewhere, TAL display a comprehensive list of over 200 AI-related patents that the company has registered (see TAL 2021d), suggesting a productive research and development capacity, but also an agenda for ownership and protection of intellectual property to accompany the open access provision. In these ways, TAL seems to have emerged as a particularly interesting kind of organisation – perhaps not exclusively as a result of the *double reduction* policy, but at least in part due to the curbing of its private education activity – positioned as a central state actor, but also comprising the capacity for innovative technical development more usually associated with the private sector. This position appears to entail significant influence and power, not only to develop sophisticated AI in response to a range of international challenges, but also to define both the form and specific internal functioning of AI systems made available to the wider education technology sector in China. Framing their role as a 'platform', TAL further describes this gatekeeping role thusly:

> By promoting supply-side reform of the education service sector, the platform strives to both increase productivity and cut the cost among education. Through breakthroughs, distribution of education resources, and realizing data-driven individualized teaching at scale, it will bring changes to educational concepts and models. Meanwhile, the

R&D threshold for small to medium enterprises, as well as the risk in commercialization for education institutions, will be lowered.

(TAL Education Group 2021b)

In other words, TAL seems poised to become a core, centralised national provider of AI applications for education in China, not only by offering research and development capacities that ostensibly outperform other private enterprises, but also through providing cost-free services for educational institutions that might otherwise struggle with the financial burden of commercial applications.

Squirrel AI, learning machines, and state schools

The third and final example of the impact of the *double reduction* examines the company Squirrel AI (also introduced in the previous chapter). While Squirrel AI differs in the size and influence of its private education activity in comparison to the previous two examples, the company nevertheless constitutes an important aspect of the broader terrain of AI and education in China, focusing on a very specific learning platform, and promoting the business internationally. As a smaller and more focused entity, Squirrel AI's response to the recent regulation offers key insights about the direction of AI development for education, as it straddles a continuing private demand and moves towards more state educational provision.

As with New Oriental and TAL, the *double reduction* policy necessitated some rather rapid responses from Squirrel AI, given that the provision of after-school private education was no longer a viable business. As discussed in the previous chapter, Squirrel AI's operations focused on a very particular market, that of second- and third-tier cities (an orientation examined again in the next chapter), in which the company's software was provided through local 'learning centres'. This arrangement meant that Squirrel AI was focused substantially on the 'learning centre' model, and that students interacting with the technology were doing so in a classroom-type setting, involving teachers and teaching assistants leading classes, as well as peer learners, undertaking combinations of whole-class activity and individualised engagement with the software. Squirrel AI's responses to the *double reduction* challenged both these dimensions, first, by developing relationships with state schools, and, second, by producing a dedicated hardware version of its adaptive learning system.

As with the previous examples, reactions to the *double reduction* have often appeared to be exercises in rebranding as much as they are in actual transformations of commercial practices. A recent article in the *China Daily* on Squirrel AI's prospects (Y. Cheng 2021) is one example, in which, presumably as a result of concerns over potentially negative repercussions for share value, the company portrays a sense of stability rather than volatility, and a business model that seems unperturbed by the recent regulation. This is a vital dimension to understand in examining the fallout from the *double reduction*, which often takes the form of businesses recasting themselves as entities that were never really in conflict with the regulation, and where the latest commercial ventures are in fact long-standing company strategies rather than reactive attempts to remain viable. Given the decimation of share value widely reported after the *double reduction*, such attempts to convey stability appear to be a vital form of subsistence for companies connected, in one form or another, to the private education sector. Importantly, this survival strategy is another key aspect of the decoupling of AI development in China from the private educational sphere, a previous association which, as argued in Chapter 3, is foundational to the ways the technology has emerged.

Squirrel AI serves as a central example of this disassociation. Mirroring the policy language examined in Chapter 2, founder of the company Li Haoyang suggests

> Educational informationization has become an inevitable trend amid the COVID-19 pandemic. More public schools are spending more money on software and services to drive information technology facilities.
>
> (Li Haoyang quoted in Y. Cheng 2021)

Here a demand for AI from the state school sector is implied, and linked to the recent pandemic, which amplified partnerships between schools and private technology companies globally (e.g. Williamson and Hogan 2020). This link to schooling is emphasised by the suggestion that Squirrel AI 'has provided public schools with digitalization and informationization services for years' (Y. Cheng 2021). The economics of Squirrel AI are further explained by framing the company, not as an organisation involved with the provision of education, but rather as a supplier of technology: 'around 93 percent of the company's revenue comes from fees for technology services while students' tuition only accounts for the rest' (Y. Cheng 2021). Here, Squirrel AI is subtly but deliberately recast as a technology company, and therefore not the kind of organisation that would have been impacted by the *double reduction*. As such, the ambiguity of an AI developer for education is brought to the fore. Whereas one might interpret Squirrel's previous commercial activity as being, at least to some extent, 'in the education business', by developing software for specific educational purposes, and leasing the technology in a franchise-type model to various learning centres (as detailed in the previous chapter), one might also interpret its enterprise as wholly technical, particularly where education technology is seen in instrumentalist terms. In other words, the boundary between what constitutes an education company as opposed to a mere developer of AI technology *applied* to educational contexts is a matter of interpretation. However, portraying such an organisation in terms of 'SaaS' (software as a service), or indeed 'AIaaS' (AI as a service), seems to negate any responsibility for the resulting educational activity, and assume that the technology is simply a product to be sold through subscription. There are implications here for the form and quality of relationships between such an organisation and its end users, educational institutions, teachers, and students, who would appear to have diminished means for contact and feedback in the SaaS model.

Squirrel AI's (re)emphasis on technology provision offers another example of the decoupling of educational AI development from the private education sector. In the same article, it is suggested that 'Squirrel AI launched its first AI intelligent adaptive learning system back in 2017. As of last year, it has served over 60,000 public schools across 1,200 cities in the nation' (Y. Cheng 2021), not only underscoring the role of service, but emphasising relationships with schools (learning centres are not mentioned at all in the article). Squirrel AI has further advertised its new partnerships with state schools across various social media channels in China, in a move which is additionally significant due to the kinds of institutions involved: just like its 'learning centre' business, these schools appear to be predominantly located in second- and third-tier cities, and in areas which lack the educational resources and teaching expertise of wealthier regions. This orientation, as will be discussed further in the next chapter, is aligned with a wider government education strategy to address inequalities between regions, and is therefore perceived as an 'acceptable' direction for AI development. Alongside a shift to providing AI services within state schools, as opposed to private learning centres, Squirrel AI began producing what it termed a 'learning machine' (see iNews 2022), in reference to a dedicated tablet device pre-loaded with the company's adaptive learning software. An announcement from electronics company TCL appears to reveal that the 'learning machine' may be a result of their collaboration with Squirrel AI (see TCL 2022). Similar to the shift to state schools, the development of hardware was designed to avoid the context of the learning centres entirely, and establish a 'direct-to-consumer' relationship with customers (that being students and presumably their parents). Li Haoyang explains this shift in economic terms, as a direct consequence of the *double reduction*:

> The education and training market will shrink from 1 trillion yuan to 300 billion yuan (with the country's regulations on the after-school tutoring market). However, the learning equipment market is expected to rise from 10 billion yuan to 200 billion yuan because for students, self-learning has become more and more important.
>
> (Li Haoyang quoted in Y. Cheng 2021)

However, the direct-to-consumer relationship, while also contributing to the disassociation of AI from private education, has broader implications than mere favourable financial prospects. While Squirrel AI's learning centres tended to provide an educational environment with many similarities to a classroom, including teachers undertaking whole-class and group teaching, in an environment with peer interaction (alongside, of course, significant time spent individually interacting with the AI software), the direct-to-consumer arrangement excises all of these potential pedagogical interactions. The use of the 'learning machine' thus transforms the educational experience with Squirrel AI into a self-directed, an ostensibly isolated, undertaking. Furthermore, such an arrangement seems to establish a completely *unregulated* form of education, in which the state has no oversight over young people's interactions with AI, or indeed their after-school study routines.

New markets for AI

Both the shift to state schools and the provision of dedicated 'smart' hardware are not unique to Squirrel AI. So-called 'smart hardware', including tablets, have risen substantially in popularity following both the *double reduction* regulation and the COVID-19 pandemic, as parents increasingly turn to support for studying at home (see One DU Finance 2021; iNews 2022). Other examples of the development of tablet devices include iFlyTek, as discussed in the previous chapter, as well as Yuanfudao (see iNews 2022), and UMeWorld, which provide English-language tuition through the brand 'Easy Learn' (see Bloomberg 2021b). As these reports also note, the combination of the *double reduction* and the pandemic has stimulated what seems to be a new kind of education technology market for hardware devices, including 'smart lamps' and 'smart pens' that appear to incorporate a wide range of data-driven features, such as voice recognition and OCR. Despite the obvious government concern about the sense of competition and pressure engendered through the private education market in China, for which the *double reduction* was primarily established, the proliferation of such hardware devices appears to have produced a completely unregulated domain of new AI-driven gadgets, and one which may greatly increase young people's daily interactions with sophisticated data-driven systems. Furthermore, the rapid rise of 'smart' devices attests to the proficiency and durability of the private sector, who seem to have capitalised on the consequences of regulation intended to ultimately manage their influence. Recent reports indicate the establishment of a new ministerial department to provide oversight of the private education sector (Ni 2021d); however, the extent to which this new market is being regulated is not yet clear. This example underscores an important sense of conflict and contestation in the differing sociotechnical imaginaries of AI proliferating in China. On the one hand, the *double reduction* policy might be understood as an example of the ways policy-driven visions of AI as a site of regulation and state control are directly shaping the ways the technology is designed and deployed. On the other, a narrative of market-driven innovation, in which AI resurfaces and transforms in response to consumer demand, appears to also be flourishing, maintained by private sector interests.

The rise of AI in state schools, however, is perhaps a more significant shift, and one that can be seen not simply as an exclusive outcome of the *double reduction* policy, but rather as a more centralised mandate incentivised through a range of policies. As examined in Chapter 2, the notions of 'informatization' and 'smart' education have been circulated in numerous policies previous to the private sector regulation, urging the development of an AI-driven ecosystem across the education sector. The key question in response to such policies was how such a vision would be achieved, and the impact from the *double reduction* appears to offer some of the answers. The reorganisations of TAL and Squirrel AI, as discussed above, suggest the establishing of centralised structural support for AI implementation (in the form of TAL's 'Open AI Platform'), as well as the increasing use of sophisticated adaptive learning systems in state schools in ways that, ostensibly, address the governments concerned for inequality (in the form of Squirrel AI's operations in lower-tier cities).

Announcements from the Ministry of Education in 2022 also call for the implementation of 'the strategic action of education digitization', involving the development of 'the "Internet + education" model' and an acceleration of 'digital transformation and [the] smart upgrade of education' (Mao 2022). There is also an announcement about the construction of a 'national smart education public service platform' and 'smart classroom development across universities, primary and secondary schools' (ibid). Such phrases unmistakably refer to AI-driven systems being positioned as central aspects of state education reform.

Concluding remarks

This chapter examined the recent *double reduction* policy and its implications of AI development. Read alongside Chapter 2, the regulation suggests an overarching shift from general incentivisation of AI, as described previously in the *National Strategy* and *Action Plan for Universities and Colleges*, towards greater state control. Thus, also following from the discussion in Chapter 2, the *double reduction* might be understood as bolstering a government-led vision of AI, in which the technology can be managed, controlled, and harnessed for the state.

The chapter described the effects of the double reduction regulation on three prominent education companies in China that are substantially involved in the development of AI: New Oriental, TAL, and Squirrel AI (introduced in the previous chapter). New Oriental's private education provision appears to have been decimated by the regulation, and the company made a radical shift to online sales, emphasising the precarity of the sector. Having already adopted a semi-government role as 'AI champion' for 'smart education', TAL appears to be focusing on an 'Open AI Platform' to support other companies with AI technologies. Thus, the regulation appears to have enticed TAL towards more of a state role. Squirrel AI announced the production of a dedicated hardware device, as well as renewed interest in the state school market, thus demonstrating the requirement for a shifting company strategy. Across all of these examples, the regulation appears to have substantially altered the design and deployment of educational AI.

As a final reflection, it may be more productive to view the *double reduction* as aligned both with a broader cluster of education policy and with other regulations related to technology also issued in 2021. The key example here is the 'Guiding Opinions on Strengthening Overall Governance of Internet Information Service Algorithms' (关于加强互联网信息服务算法综合治理的指导意见), hereafter GOSOGIISA (see CAC 2021), which was reported widely in the media outside of China and interpreted as 'curbing the power of the big tech platforms' and 'the world's most ambitious effort to regulate artificial intelligence' (Conrad and Knight 2022). The policy included measures to prevent addiction to social media content, prevent the use of personal data to determine individual pricing, and provide the ability for internet users to opt out of algorithmic recommendation systems. However, as has been a key theme across this book so far, perceiving this policy in isolation, and as a sudden 'crackdown' on 'big tech', provides an impoverished view. Rather than simply aimed at curbing the power of prominent technology companies, the policy is better understood as part of a much broader regulatory push, not only to maintain governance, but to actively utilise AI technology for social security and stability. This is where a return to the conceptual framing of sociotechnical imaginaries is useful, allowing such policies to be considered in terms of the broader future visions of technology that they imply. Here, both the *double reduction* and the GOSOGIISA might be understood as aligned under a wider imaginary of AI technology in service to the state, which functions by pulling private sector innovation closer to national priorities. Returning to Lin's (2006) triadic framework, such attempts to manage the novel functioning of powerful data-driven technologies can be understood within the broader attempts to hold together nationalism, socialism, and developmentalism, where private sector innovation with AI may have been perceived as overly focused on the latter. The state's imaginary of AI, therefore, appears to infer the technology's potential to induce a moral vacuum, unless guided and managed by a central authority.

Notes

1 'Artificial Intelligence Open Innovation Platform' is perhaps a better translation of the 'AI Champion' initiative, indicating the specific role played by the identified organisations, and particularly TAL, in the provision of open access to both AI services and data.
2 Organisers of the 2020 challenge are listed as Aleix M. Martinez, Ohio State University; Sergio Escalera, Universitat de Barcelona; Qianli Feng, Ohio State University.

References

Alpaydin, E. (2016). *Machine Learning: the new AI.* Cambridge: MIT Press.

Bloomberg. (2021a). Under Siege, China EdTech giants take steps to curb fallout. *Bloomberg.* 28 July https://www.bloomberg.com/news/articles/2021-07-28/under-siege-china-s-edtech-giants-take-steps-to-contain-fallout

Bloomberg. (2021b). UMeWorld unveils new business model for its easy learn ai-powered English learning centers in southern China. *Bloomberg.* 6 October. https://www.bloomberg.com/press-releases/2021-10-06/umeworld-unveils-new-business-model-for-its-easy-learn-ai-powered-english-learning-centers-in-southern-china

Bloomberg News. (2021). Under Siege, China EdTech giants take steps to curb fall-out. *Bloomberg News.* 29 July. https://finance.yahoo.com/news/under-siege-china-edtech-giants-111141411.html?guccounter=1

Cao, A. (2022). New Oriental's Yu Minhong brings back English teaching with a live-streaming e-commerce twist. *South China Morning Post.* 11 June. Available: https://www.scmp.com/tech/big-tech/article/3181342/new-orientals-yu-minhong-brings-back-english-teaching-live-streaming

CAC [Cyberspace Administration of China]. (2021). (Translation by Katharin Tai and Rogier Creemers) Guiding opinions on strengthening overall governance of internet information service algorithms. https://digichina.stanford.edu/work/translation-guiding-opinions-on-strengthening-overall-governance-of-internet-information-service-algorithms/

Che, C. (2021). China's after-school tutoring crackdown goes nuclear. *Sup-China.* 23 July. https://supchina.com/2021/07/23/chinas-after-school-tutoring-crackdown-goes-nuclear/

Chen, J. (2021). (In Chinese) Ministry of education: 97.5% of parents are satisfied with the effect of reducing burden and improving quality in the new semester. *The Paper.* 23 September. Available: https://www.thepaper.cn/newsDetail_forward_14622154

Cheng, E. (2021). Another group of U.S.-listed China stocks plunge as Beijing regulators crack down. *CNBC.* 23 July https://www.cnbc.com/2021/07/23/us-listed-china-education-stocks-plunge-as-beijing-regulators-crack-down.html

Cheng, Y. (2021). Education tech firm Squirrel AI bullish on market prospects. *China Daily.* 16 September. Available: https://www.chinadaily.com.cn/a/202109/16/WS6142fa9ca310e0e3a6822120.html

Conrad, J., & Knight, W. (2022). China is about to regulate AI—and the world is watching. *Wired.* 22 February. https://www.wired.com/story/china-regulate-ai-world-watching/

Du, X. (2021). Beijing to offer jobs for those affected by education crackdown. *Sixth Tone.* 18 August. Available: https://www.sixthtone.com/news/1008284

EmotioNet Challenge. (2019). EmotioNet challenge. http://cbcsl.ece.ohio-state.edu/cvpr-2020/people.html

iNews. (2022). Smart hardware sales soar, and digital transformation of educational institutions becomes an outlet. 22 June. Available: https://inf.news/en/news/b35754f0275a21235540e726016c21e8.html

Larsen, B.C. (2019). China's national AI team: The role of National AI open inno-vation platforms. In AI Policy and China: Realities of State-Led Development, G. Webster (Ed.). Stanford-New America Digichina Project Special Report No. 1. pp. 21–25. https://newamerica.org/documents/4353/DigiChina-AI-report-20191029.pdf

Li, J. (2021). An education billionaire is going back to his rural roots after China's tutoring crackdown. Quartz. 22 December. Available: https://qz.com/2090102/new-oriental-founder-yu-minhong-is-trying-to-find-a-new-lifeline/

Li, L. (2022). [In Chinese] 双语带货爆火 新东方转型 "翻红" Outlook new era. Available: https://www.lwxsd.com/pc/info_view.php?tab=mynews&VID=25153

Liu, Y. (2021). (In Chinese). After the end of the K12 era, please don't forget to pay attention to where the thousands of education and gold diggers go. *36Kr.com*. 5 August. Available: https://36kr.com/p/1341652774098951

Ma, R. (2021). End of an era as China puts an end to for-profit tutoring companies. *The Report*. 26 July. https://www.classcentral.com/report/china-regulates-tutoring-companies/

Mao, X. (2022). Key priorities of ministry of education in 2022. *British Council*. 28 February. https://education-services.britishcouncil.org/news/market-news/key-priorities-of-ministry-of-education-2022

MEPRC [Ministry of Education of the People's Republic of China]. (2021). The general office of the central committee of the communist party of China and the general office of the state council issued the "Opinions on Further Reducing the Burden of Students' Homework and Off-campus Training in Compulsory Education". 24 July 2021. http://www.moe.gov.cn/jyb_xwfb/gzdt_gzdt/s5987/202107/t20210724_546566.html

Ni, D. (2021a). China's tutoring ban leaves a trail of debt, anger, and broken dreams. *Sixth Tone*. 1 November. https://www.sixthtone.com/news/1008838

Ni, D. (2021b) A is for anxiety: Tutoring clampdown tests China's parents. *Sixth Tone*. 27 August. https://www.sixthtone.com/news/1008347

Ni, D. (2021c). China takes tough approach to tame tutoring schools. *Sixth Tone*. 26 July https://www.sixthtone.com/news/1008085

Ni, D. (2021d). New department to oversee China's chaotic tutoring market. *Sixth Tone*. 16 June https://www.sixthtone.com/news/1007759

One DU Finance. (2021). (In Chinese) 智能学习硬件赛道火热，疯狂涌入的玩家能否如愿? Blue Whale Finance. https://lanjinger.com/d/163317

TAL. (2021a). TAL education + AI solutions. https://ai.100tal.com/

TAL. (2021b). TAL dress detection. https://ai.100tal.com/product/vu-lsda

TAL. (2021c). TAL's AI team award patent information. https://ai.100tal.com/infos/infoDetails

TAL. (2021d). TAL patents. https://ai.100tal.com/infos/infoDetailsTable?type=patents

TAL Education Group. (2021a). TAL education group provides updates on business operations. *PR Newswire*. Available: https://www.prnewswire.com/news-releases/tal-education-group-provides-updates-on-business-operations-301423024.html

TAL Education Group. (2021b). TAL's AI team wins championship award at a top international academic contest. *PR Newswire*. Available: https://www.prnewswire.com/news-releases/tals-ai-team-wins-championship-award-at-a-top-international-academic-contest-301044879.html

TCL. (2022). TCL provides enriched educational experiences for all at CES 2022, including the company's first windows laptop. *PR Newswire*. Available: https://www.prnewswire.com/news-releases/tcl-provides-enriched-educational-experiences-for-all-at-ces-2022-including-the-companys-first-windows-laptop-301453430.html

Wang, P., Wang, Z., Ji, Z., Liu, X., Yang, S., & Wu, Z. (2020). TAL EmotioNet challenge (2020). Rethinking the model chosen problem in multi-task learning. *Arxiv.* Available: https://doi.org/10.48550/arXiv.2004.09862

Wernberg-Tougaard, E. (2021). China experience. China's AI champions. Available: https://www.china-experience.com/china-experience-insights/chinas-ai-champions

Williamson, B., & Hogan, A. (2020). Commercialisation and privatisation in/of education in the context of COVID-19. *Education International.* Available https:// issuu.com/educationinternational/docs/2020_eiresearch_gr_commercialisation_ privatisation?fr=sZDJkYjE1ODA2MTQ

Wu, P. (2021, November 10). New oriental is switching from teaching english to selling vegetables. *Sixth Tone.* https://www.sixthtone.com/news/1008928

Xi, Wang Xue. (2022). https://bcc.xiwang.com/

Xue, H. (2021). Why time's up for China's 'shadow education' industry. *Sixth Tone.* 7 August. Available: https://www.sixthtone.com/news/1008175

Zhang. (2022). Livestreaming sparks hope for new oriental. *China Daily.* 16 June. Available: https://global.chinadaily.com.cn/a/202206/16/WS62aa690ea310fd2b29e62f21. html

5 Cities, regions, and rural divides

Following from the previous three chapters, which have examined relationships between the state and the private sector in the expansion and governance of artificial intelligence (AI) and education in China, this chapter aims to situate these developments within broader regional dynamics and the wider political and geographic composition of the country. Just as the previous chapters have sought to challenge assumptions about the monolithic, hierarchical, and centralised government in China as well as simplistic relationships between state and private enterprise, the focus in this chapter on foregrounding regional structures and networks offers an important additional sense of the emerging distributed governance of AI. City development will be shown to be central in the imaginaries for AI development, as government funding, local infrastructure, collaborating universities, and vibrant start-up companies come together in productive urban networks and hubs. While AI technology itself often appears to be portrayed as without context, emerging from some kind of pure scientific endeavour or a benevolent desire to solve social and educational challenges, situating such developments within actual places, relations, and locations offers an important sense of understanding how data-driven technologies emerge in particular ways. The chapter will begin with an examination of Zhongguancun, often hailed as the origins of China's technology sector, and an imagined model for government-endorsed urban centres of entrepreneurship and innovation elsewhere in the country. The area therefore constitutes an important imaginary about the ways a creative private sector can build a utopic ecosystem of commercial AI development, by co-locating businesses, academic research, and university education. Embedded in this vision, but often less acknowledged, is the role of the university, which will be explored below as occupying a key place in the broader imaginaries of the urban networks that drive AI development. Universities are positioned as institutions which advance AI development through partnerships between research institutes and private technology companies, often alongside the offering of AI-related skills training and qualifications. As will be detailed below, the geographical proximity of top-tier educational institutions and leading technologies companies in key cities, along with local government

DOI: 10.4324/9781003375135-5

organisations committed to advancing national policy (as discussed in Chapter 2), combine to make urban space particularly prominent in China's wider narratives of AI development.

However, the relationships between AI and education do not begin and end in cities, and indeed it is their very prominence that indicates a much deeper geographical context, to which the second part of this chapter turns. The prosperity of cities in the eastern coastal regions points to what is perhaps the most important dynamic in China: a rural and urban divide, generally separating wealthier regions on the east coast from poorer inland regions to the west. As will be examined further below, one might see China as continuing to be constituted from the transitions between rural and urban societies, engineered through various political projects and commercial activity, and directly producing the (unequal) societal contexts for which education and AI are often positioned as solutions. Perhaps first and foremost, these relationships highlight a crucially important sense of regional difference across China, as a useful counter to assumptions about a homogenous and centrally controlled Chinese state. The dominance of wealthier cities and regions demonstrates the vastly different ways in which China's 'national' policy on AI is being implemented (Hine 2022). However, such regional dynamics also point to the importance of recent political history in China, through which various government programmes have sought to both boost urbanisation and raise up rural areas, underpinned by a drive to develop industry, the economy, and science and technology. It is vital to understand contemporary ambitions for AI in China through this 20th-century context, not only, as will be detailed below, where specific technologies are designed and developed explicitly for rural and less-developed populations, but also where AI-oriented curricular is positioned as a solution to the country's shifting industry and employment opportunities. Long-standing urban and rural inequalities continue to animate the ways AI and education is designed and developed, and this chapter offers a historical, political, and geographical background to specific contemporary developments in the relationships between AI and education in China, therefore suggesting crucial contexts through which particular entrepreneurial and regulatory practices might be better understood.

Zhongguancun: the 'spiritual home' of China's technology industry

If there is a spiritual home for the technology sector in China, it is undoubtedly Zhongguancun (中关村), located in the Haidian district, or Haidian Qu (海淀区), northwest of Beijing. Lee describes Zhongguancun as the 'Silicon Valley of China' and 'the beating heart of China's AI movement' (2018, p3). It was technology entrepreneurs in this area, so Lee argues, that were directly inspired by the so-called 'Sputnik moment' of AlphaGo's victories in the game of Go (detailed in Chapter 2), an event that 'lit a fire under the Chinese technology community that has been burning ever since' (2018, p3). The area is frequently cited as the originator and inspiration for China's current focus on urban 'zones' directed towards science and technology development (Gao et al. 2015; Slater 2018; Dong et al. 2019), and the ultimate example of localising Chinese networks of entrepreneurial creativity and expertise (Lee 2018). In this way Zhongguancun itself is enveloped in the wider sociotechnical imaginaries of AI in China, as a site of pure innovation, through which the technology can develop authentically as a product of technical expertise and entrepreneurial creativity.

However, examining Zhongguancun's history reveals distinctly academic origins. This further demonstrates the important underlying and historical links between private sector innovation and the public education system in China. As Dong et al. (2019) note, during the Republic era, two universities – Tsinghua University and Yenching University – were built in the area (the campus of the latter subsequently becoming the home of Peking University). Further, after the founding of the People's Republic of China (PRC), Zhongguancun[1] was identified specifically as the capital's cultural and educational district, which precipitated the establishing of 'a large number of universities and scientific research institutions' (Dong et al. 2019) in the area, including the Chinese Academy of Sciences. Given this early focus on scientific research, Zhongguancun was well placed to respond to the market reforms of 1978, as discussed previously. Chunxian Chen, a member of the Institute of Physics at the Chinese Academy of Sciences, is credited with launching the first non-government entity in Zhongguancun in 1980, entitled the 'Advanced Technology Service Association' (Sullivan and Liu-Sullivan 2015), establishing a trend for businesses being founded in partnership with various academic institutes and computer science departments in the area throughout the 1980s (see Dong et al. 2019). This connection between start-up companies and universities is still apparent in the development of AI today, as discussed previously. Towards the end of the 1980s, the area became known as 'Electronics Street' (Dong et al. 2019), due to the spread of companies producing technologies of various kinds, as well as the proliferation of electronics marketplaces that became established in the area (Chen 2020). Chen notes how the area developed a reputation as the 'go-to place' for 'any type of tech device' and a 'retail tech paradise' (2020, n.p.). Two significant events occurred in Zhongguancun in 1987 that are worthy of note here. In April of that year, the first invention patent application was submitted, relating to Chinese character font generation, establishing the culture of innovation and entrepreneurship that the area has subsequently become known for. Five months later in September, Zhongguancun became the site of China's very first email, sent by Wang Yunfeng and Li Chengjiong of the Chinese Academy of Sciences to colleagues at Karlsruhe University in Germany (Hauben 2010),[2] initiating the era of networked technologies that would radically alter the direction of technology development. According to Dong et al., the email read: 'across the Great Wall we can reach every corner in the world' (2019, p4), perhaps setting a precedent for China's AI visions 30 years later.

Alongside additional and significant enterprise and financial development in the area, which, according to Dong et al. employed 'more than 5,000 people and generated a total revenue of more than 900 million RMB' (2019, p4), these events encouraged a shift in the governance of Zhongguancun, away from the designations of culture and education, and towards the establishment of the 'Beijing New Technology Industrial Development Trial Zone' in 1988 (Gao et al. 2015). Zhongguancun thus became the 'first high-tech park in China' (Gao et al. 2015, p1057), and with this 'experimental' status, began a rapid phase of growth. It was in this period that the New Oriental School was founded by Yu Minhong in central Zhongguancun on 16 November 1993, a company that would later become New Oriental Education Technology in 2001, not only the biggest private education business in China, but also a key player in the early development of educational AI, as examined in Chapters 3 and 4. It was undoubtedly the company's location within Zhongguancun that provided the incentives and capacities to develop towards data-driven technologies.

In 1998, the first example of private capital investment was established through the founding of Zhongguancun Science and Technology Investment Co. (Dong et al. 2019), signalling the rise of the area as a significant site of private economic activity. The 'trial' period came to an end just one year later, as the area officially became 'Zhongguancun Science Park', with the aim of establishing:

> a national science and technology innovation demonstration base with international competitiveness, a base for incubating and radiating scientific and technological achievements in the nation, and a training base for high-quality creative talents.
>
> (Dong et al. 2019, p9)

Thus, aligned with China's rapidly developing economy in the 1990s as discussed previously, the strategic governance of 'Zhongguancun Science Park' began to shift into a discourse of outward-facing, international comparison and competitiveness, situating the area as a technology hub on the world stage. This outlook was further solidified through a new designation in 2009: 'Zhongguancun National Innovation Demonstration Zone' (Gao et al. 2015), with a specific remit for 'independent innovation' and 'global influence' (Dong et al. 2019, p12). It was in this period that foreign technology companies, such as Microsoft, Google, and Intel, established regional headquarters and research centres in the area (Chen 2020). Significantly, for Chen, this era signalled the end of Zhongguancun's previous reputation as a marketplace for electronics goods, suggesting of this time: 'aged electronics markets are phased out while new cohorts of entrepreneurs are establishing their first startup offices' (2020, n.p.).

Lee (2018) identifies this transition in 2009 as the beginnings of Zhongguancun's key role in AI development. Emphasising the instrumental role of government official Guo Hong, Lee describes plans to adapt the 'abstract cultural zeitgeist' of Silicon Valley in the US to function within the 'physical realities of present-day China' (2018, p53):

> Silicon Valley's ecosystem had taken shape organically over several decades. But what if we in China could speed up that process by brute-forcing the geographic proximity? We could pick one street in Zhongguancun, clear out all the old inhabitants, and open the space to key players in this kind of ecosystem: VC firms, startups, incubators, and service providers.

This link between government strategy and geographical proximity is key to understanding the ways AI has been developed in China. State incentivisation, described as 'an unprecedented wave of government support for innovation' (Lee 2018, p54), often materialised in the form of urban zones dedicated to technology and entrepreneurial activity, with Zhongguancun as the model. As Lee describes, this began with substantial shifts in the Chinese internet around 2013, which, through the development of a range of innovative apps such as WeChat, took on a character and an economy of its own, with entrepreneurial activity in Zhongguancun leading the development of technologies designed specifically for Chinese contexts. Huge volumes of data circulating in the Chinese internet hailed 'an overnight boom in production of the natural resource of the AI age' (Lee 2018, p53). Many of China's biggest technology companies, such as Baidu, emerged from Zhongguancun through this period. Launching their search engine in 2001, Baidu was listed on the New York Stock Exchange in 2004, becoming 'Nasdaq's first Chinese Internet company with a market capitalization of over 100 billion RMB' (Dong et al. 2019, p11). As also discussed in the next chapter, Baidu has emerged as a key player in the development of AI, precisely due to its dominant position in internet search, and hence an ability to harvest data. Baidu was designated a 'national AI champion' for autonomous driving (see Larsen 2019), and formed many partnerships with universities overseas, emerging as a prominent developer of AI-related school curriculum and educational resources, discussed further in Chapter 6. Furthermore, it was not just specific companies that expanded and transformed due to their successes within the local networks of Haidian district, but Zhongguancun itself. Zhongguancun 'is now a concept as much as a place' (Economist 2019), having not only become a byword for urban technology zones in other areas of China, but also used as the title for other science and innovations parks within Beijing. Indeed, Lee's (2018) imaginary for an AI-infused Chinese education detailed in the introduction to this book is articulated as a key culmination of the creative entrepreneurial spirit forged in Zhongguancun, and now supposedly disseminated across China. It is in this way that Zhongguancun forms a key dimension of China's vision of AI-driven futures, by including a sense of place in the narrative of innovation, and a utopic imaginary of intensive urban agglomeration.

While Lee's (2018) account of Zhongguancun's transformation provides important detail about the national and local contexts through which a specifically 'Chinese' technology industry, eventually involving AI, took place, it also reveals the deep ties with Silicon Valley, and between China and the US. In 2009, Kai-Fu Lee had himself returned to China from a distinguished career with some of the biggest technology companies in the US, including Apple, Microsoft, and Google. Drawing on this experience, as suggested above, Kai-Fu Lee, alongside many other technology entrepreneurs who had either been educated or worked in the US, viewed Silicon Valley as the ultimate source of inspiration for China's growth, and the specific model for Zhongguancun's development as a hub for innovation. It is important, therefore, to emphasise that, at least from the perspective of the those developing technologies in places such as Zhongguancun, the relationship between China and the US is not necessarily one of rivalry and geopolitical positioning, but rather of profound connection. Moreover, as Lee (2018) emphasises, the post-2009 era of Zhongguancun was defined by a shift in orientation to developing internet technologies designed very specifically for Chinese markets and contexts, and therefore Silicon Valley represented a set of ideas for innovation that could be drawn upon to create new opportunities in China. In this sense, Silicon Valley can be understood, not in opposition to a place such as Zhongguancun, but rather as a model that might be rearticulated and reapplied to a different national context.

Of course, this doesn't mean that national policy-makers in China necessarily took the same view, and the government backing of urban science and technology hubs can certainly be understood as part of broader geopolitical strategy, with a distinct nationalistic emphasis. In contrast to the emphasis on the entrepreneurial spirit of the private sector emphasised by figures such as Kai-Fu Lee, it is state backing that is often emphasised elsewhere. Roberts et al., for example, describe Zhongguancun as:

> a purpose-built, government subsidised, incubator workspace that provides a suite of services to help Chinese technology start-ups succeed, often in the sectors where national champions have been selected.
>
> (Roberts et al. 2021, p61)

This reflects one of the key tensions explored across this book – that of the relationships between the state and the private sector in the development of AI in China – but also the divergent interpretations often encountered from Chinese and Western perspectives. While Chinese accounts often seem to attribute little significance to combinations of state funding and private sector activity, Western reports often tend to suggest something of an unfair advantage in government involvement. Nevertheless, the 'national champions' referenced above are a key example of such collaborations, as examined in the previous chapter's discussion of Tomorrow Advancing Life (TAL) and their transformation into an 'AI platform' for 'smart education'.

While differences over what might constitute authentic relationships between the state and the private sector get to the heart of the foundational political and ideological distinctions between China and the West, the focus on national comparisons and geopolitical contestation, as argued elsewhere, tends to overlook the significance of education. For some, Zhongguancun is the embodiment of creative entrepreneurial fervour, while for others it may be a symbol of 'top down' state intervention, but it is less commonly interpreted in terms of its academic foundations and educational connections. Gao et al. suggest Zhongguancun to be 'the most intensive scientific, education and talent resource base in China' (2015, p1057). This intensity is further explained through the proximity of key actors in the area:

> 40 colleges and universities like Peking University and Tsinghua University, more than 200 national (municipal) scientific institutions such as the Chinese Academy of Sciences and the Chinese Academy of Engineering, 67 state-level laboratories, 27 national engineering research centers, 28 national engineering and technological research centers, 24 university S & T [science and technology] parks and 29 overseas student pioneer parks.
>
> (Gao et al. 2015, p1057).

It is precisely through these conditions that a 'model for Industry-University-Institution Alliance' (Gao et al. 2015, p1057) has provided Zhongguancun with the capacity to adopt a leading role in the recent development of AI. Education is more typically positioned as the entry point to the entrepreneurial activities of a site such as Zhongguancun, for example, as suggested by *The Economist*: '[a]rmed with capital, a new company can stake out office space easily and quickly, and tap into annually refreshed stocks of technically minded graduates from the most prestigious universities in Beijing' (2019). However, as suggested in this section, educational institutions form a much more integral part of Zhongguancun, having a formal role in its origins, but also continuing to develop the area as a site of expertise, not simply in supplying graduates, but also by partnering with companies to drive forward research and development.

University AI power

While government incentivisation and entrepreneurial fervour are often emphasised in accounts of China's AI development, educational institutions, and universities in particular, deserve more attention as key elements of the visions of national strategy and technological development. This section will suggest that universities are imagined as powerful actors within the political economy of AI, assumed not only to provide research expertise for the networks and collaborations that are driving forward government policy at the local level, but also to be emerging as international hubs of 'talent' that advance China's geopolitical agenda for technological ascendency. The discussion of this latter aspect will also be continued into the next chapter. For now, it is important to examine the ways universities are envisioned as functioning within the regional contexts of China. Universities, as suggested above, are positioned as key components in the emergence of entrepreneurial start-up activity, but also central to the subsequent advancement of technical fields, as private companies seek to develop collaborations with research centres and computer science departments to advance the knowledge of AI. In this sense, education, in the form of universities that support and prioritise research, might be seen as being at the very centre of the current sociotechnical imaginary of AI in China. As will be detailed in the next chapter, such universities are being positioned, not just as producers of cutting-edge AI research that can be commercialised through external partnerships, but also as centres of reformed curricula that prioritise the kind of technical skills assumed to be required for the future data-driven economy. In other words, it is both in research and in teaching that universities are being depicted as central elements in China's push for AI ascendency.

Government policy is explicit about the central importance of universities, for example, in the *Education Informatization 2.0 Action Plan*, which declares that '[c]olleges and universities are at the juncture of the first productivity of science and technology, the first resource of talents, and the first driving force of innovation' (MEPRC 2018). It is precisely in this way that universities are being positioned as foundational elements of national AI development. One of the key strategic initiatives for Chinese universities in recent years has been the 'double first-class university' (双一流大学) project, first announced in 2015 (Li 2018). The term is used to describe elite universities in China which are designated as 'world first-class' institutions, as well as developing 'first-level disciplines', hence the 'double' designation. The 'double first class university' ostensibly replaced the previous Project 211 (introduced in 1995) and Project 985 (introduced in 1998) initiatives, which sought to both identify and develop China's premier academic institutions. In 2017, 42 universities were elected as 'double first class', in a move that allowed the government to focus its support on a fewer number of elite institutions to the previous Project 985, and direct institutional governance towards state strategy (Liu 2018). As Liu suggests, the 'double first class' initiative was launched against a 'background of global competition in science and technology' through which the government could focus 'on world-class universities and disciplines with greater precision' (Li 2018). As such, the 'double first class' initiative has become one of the foundations of China's broad AI strategy (Peterson et al. 2021), allowing the government to steer elite universities towards research and education development that raises their ranking on the world stage. Peterson et al. describe the initiative as a 'major push in AI education' (2021, p8), particularly for the development of an AI curriculum, and the cultivation of expertise – this is examined further in the next chapter on AI 'talent'. Subsequently, the list of 'double class universities' was raised to 147 (MEPRC 2022).

The location of the 'double first class' universities, perhaps unsurprisingly, reflects established urban centres in China. When the initial 42 were announced, Beijing hosted eight of these elite universities, while there were four in Shanghai, two in Guangzhou, two in Tianjin, and two in Nanjing. Further, 22 of these initial 'double first class' universities were located in the wealthier and more developed eastern coastal provinces (including Beijing). While the list of 'double first class' universities expanded significantly to 147 by early 2022 (MEPRC 2022), the emphasis on established cities appears to remain. Beijing hosts 34, with 15 in Shanghai, 13 in Nanjing, 7 in Guangzhou, and 6 in Tianjin (ibid). Further, 88 of the 147 are located in the eastern coastal regions (including Beijing) (ibid), appearing to indicate that government efforts to focus the strategic development of AI through elite universities is substantially oriented towards already established regions of urban development. Large cities in central regions, however, are also hosts to many of these elite institutions, such as Changsha (4), Wuhan (7), and Xi'an (7) (ibid). Further west, Chengdu in Sichuan province and neighbouring Chongqing are the sites of 7 and 2, respectively. While the emphasis is clearly in eastern regions, the latest list of 'double first class' universities appears to be shifting towards addressing this inequality, with institutions included in China's poorest western regions of Gansu, Guizhou, Yunnan, Qinghai, Tibet, and Xinjiang (ibid).

The location of the 'double first class' universities also correlates with the development of 'high tech' zones, of which Zhongguancun, examined above, was the first (Slater 2018). These areas have expanded greatly since 2010, and include zones with national-level endorsement, as well as local government initiatives, all aimed at developing technology industries (ibid). As Slater's (2018) mapping demonstrates, these zones are clustered around key eastern cities, such as Guangzhou and Shenzhen, Shanghai and Nanjing, as well as the central cities of Changsha, Wuhan, and Xi'an, and Chengdu and Chongqing further west. Therefore, while the 'high tech' zones are explicit sites of national and local government incentivisation and funding, it is notable that they are often accompanied by elite universities that are also a focus of centralised strategic priorities in technology development. While not all of these 'high tech' zones are necessarily focused on AI, there are indications that the technology will also be the focus of new urban developments. Baruzzi notes the announcement of eight new 'AI innovation zones', 'where specific technologies are developed based on the city's features, which will complement the strategy adopted at the national level for the area where the city is located' (2021). The 'AI innovation zones' appear to align with the urban emphasis discussed above, with seven being located in key cities within eastern coastal regions, specifically Beijing, Tianjin, Jinan-Qingdao,

Shanghai, Hangzhou, Shenzhen, Guangzhou (ibid). The only zone outside these regions is the one announced in Chengdu, which, as noted above, is also a key location for 'double first class' universities. Indeed, all eight of the new 'AI innovation zones' are in cities with these elite institutions, further demonstrating the formal link between universities, government incentivisation, and private enterprise that is driving the development of AI in China.

One of the key ways in which higher educational institutions are contributing to the broader strategy for AI development is through the formation of dedicated AI institutes, which serve as a focus of research activity, industry collaboration, and education development (Peterson et al. 2021). Peterson et al. suggest that 'at least 34 institutions launched their own AI institutes between 2017–2018' (2021, p13) as a direct response to the announcement of the national AI policy around the same time, as discussed in Chapter 2. Elite universities were quick to respond to the incentivisation, including the launch of an AI institute at Shanghai Jiao Tong University (Ke 2018), and the announcement of the development of an entire new 68.35-hectare campus of Peking University devoted to AI (Du 2018). As Peterson et al. (2021) emphasise, such institutes are often the result of industry partnerships, for example, between AI unicorn iFlyTek and Chongqing University of Posts and Telecommunications Center for Security and Emerging Technology, set up in in 2018. Tencent is also given as an example, establishing AI institutes in the same year with Shandong University of Science and Technology and Liaoning Technical University (Peterson et al. 2021). Importantly, therefore, universities become key sites of AI activity, drawing in private sector expertise and resources, and acting as centres for research and education that develop a particular locality. As with the Zhongguancun model described above, universities generate expertise that can supply local companies as well as provide established businesses with a means to extend their AI capabilities through research. While the next chapter will explore the generation of AI 'talent' further, it is crucial to examine where AI institutes are being established. As Peterson et al.'s (2021) analysis demonstrates, there is a striking distinction between East and West China in terms of the prevalence of university AI institutes. All 12 eastern coastal provinces (including Beijing and Shanghai), from Guangdong and Fujian in the south to Jilin and Heilongjiang in the north, have at least one AI institute, while almost every province to the west of these areas, apart from the central provinces of Shaanxi, Hubei, and Chongqing, have none. If there is a 'university power' related to the development of AI, it appears to be conditioned by China's regional geography, and it is to this broad set of historical issues that the final section of the chapter will turn. The distinct lack of AI institutes in Central and Western China suggests substantial inequality in the way regional development, and the subsequent benefits to the local economy, will emerge across the country. According to the imaginary of AI development, data-driven technology will not only provide opportunities for individual employment in the emerging AI industry, but also provide the products to improve all manner of societal inefficiencies. However, where sites of AI advancement become clustered around existing regions of socio-economic advantage, the technology appears to offer the prospect of exacerbating existing inequalities, rather than resolving them.

Rural inequalities and 'special economic zones'

While much of the current interest in China's AI strategy focuses on recent infrastructure projects, such as the urban 'zones' discussed above, and visions of local combinations of government funding, entrepreneurial creativity, and academic expertise, these initiatives might be better understood through an examination of broader geographical and historical contexts. In particular, the relationships between rural and urban China, as well as among western and eastern regions, are crucially important for understanding, not only the modern development of the country and its connections to educational reform, but also the ways contemporary AI and education are being imagined.

Contemporary China has a complex relationship with the country-side. In many ways the Chinese 20th century can be understood in terms of a profound shift from rural to urban populations, and the over-whelming societal changes that were initiated as a result (Kleinman et al. 2011). As the government often emphasises, modern China has suc-cessfully alleviated unprecedented levels of absolute poverty, which was overwhelming in rural regions, like no other nation in history (Brown 2020). As Brown (2020) notes, this was largely due to policy changes in the 1980s under the Chinese Communist Party (CPC) paramount leader Deng Xiaop-ing and Party Secretary Hu Yaobang, focused on decentralised governance and the authorisation of local enterprises (see also Kleinman et al. 2011). However, rural populations have been historically marginalised, and a sub-stantial inequality remains. This is a substantial source of tension, given that it was largely rural populations that were responsible for bringing the CPC to power in 1949, yet it was the countryside that was often overlooked in subsequent strategies for national development (Lin 2006; Brown 2020). As Lin (2006) suggests, this was a necessary condition for China's path of socialist modernisation:

> What stood out in terms of internal constraints was, above all, the primitive accumulation of capital through sacrificing rural develop-ment and exploiting the peasantry. This was the case fundamentally because the socialist state possessed neither colonies along with a global trade network (in contrast to early capitalist development in Europe) nor the means to borrow from the advanced economies. Thus, in order to sustain an internally generated high accumulation rate, wages and consumption had to be suppressed and the countryside subordinated to urban demands.
>
> (Lin 2006, p66)

It was precisely this system which 'enabled a rapid process of industrial growth and the construction of cities' (Lin 2006, p67) during the early years of the CPC. While the focus on industrialisation under Mao Zedong established urban areas as privileged sites of development, rural China was still perceived with a sense of socialist authenticity. In this era, urban students were often sent to the countryside for education, where communal life was seen as an idyllic form of existence to which city populations should aspire.

While the market-reform period after 1978 undoubtedly maintained the emphasis on cities as key sites for economic generation, the most profound impact of the 'opening up' policies was in rural areas (Brown 2020). As Brown contends, due to the authorisation of rural enterprises '[a] country which had experienced mass famine within a generation was, by the mid-1980s, producing enough surpluses to feed itself comfortably and export agricultural produce' (Brown 2020, p84). Nevertheless, key to the transition between Maoist socialism and the marketisation of Deng Xiaoping were the experimental 'Special Economic Zones' (SEZs), designed to contain and control capitalist activities within identified areas. However, the strategic purpose of the SEZs was, as Brown (2020) contends, to gain both revenue and the transfer of technologies from international trading partners, in exchange for cheap labour. From such a perspective, the SEZs might be understood as a precursor to the contemporary 'high tech' zones, and indeed the special 'AI innovation zones', in the sense that the Chinese government used these locations to focus the development of strategic priorities, and benefit from the proximity of advanced technology and vibrant markets. However, while the SEZs were clearly positioned for China to gain access to the more advanced technologies of (largely Western) trading partners, the contemporary 'high tech' and 'AI innovation' zones are oriented much more towards internal, domestic development, and the dissemination of Chinese technical expertise. Moreover, it now appears to be Western nations that are keen to benefit from the Chinese sources of AI 'talent' that circulate and develop in such zones – the announcement of Google's AI lab in 2017 appeared to exemplify this reversal of fortunes, with the company stating, 'we want to work with the best AI talent, wherever that talent is' (Vincent 2017).

The SEZs of the early 1980s were, for Brown, an embodiment of the key ideological shift in the market-reform period, encapsulated in a phrase derived from the Third Plenum of the Eleventh Party Congress, held in 1978: 'practice is the sole criterion for testing the truth' (2020, p77). In other words, the correct path for China – and a China framed, as Lin (2006) reminds us, in terms of nationalism, socialism, and developmentalism – was to be determined, not by strict adherence to Marxist dogma, but through pragmatic experimentation. The most significant of the SEZs was Shenzhen, with its close proximity to Hong Kong, at the time under the control of the UK. Brown describes its rapid growth thusly:

> Tower blocks and vast new industrial zones and residential areas appeared. The influx of a new class of people, migrant workers,

recruited from outside in order to come to work in these immense new enterprises, meant the town almost in a matter of years became a city, growing to a million by the early 1990s, and then 6 million by the turn of the millennium … If anywhere exemplified capitalism with Chinese characteristics, this was the place.

(Brown 2020, p86)

Since Deng Xiaoping famously visited Shenzhen in the early 1990s as a symbolic reaffirmation of the CPC's commitment to marketisation, the site has come to represent the successes of 'reform with Chinese characteristics' (Brown 2020, p87). As Brown also notes, Xi Jinping visited in 2012, 'within weeks of being appointed Party Secretary' (2020, p87), and again in 2018. In addition, there was much media coverage of his visit in 2020 to mark the 40th anniversary of the Shenzhen SEZ (e.g. Au 2020). For Brown, Shenzhen is thus one of the 'hallowed spaces of the new China' (2020 p86) and 'sacred sites for reform and opening up' (2020, p149). It is perhaps no surprise that Shenzhen is now a key focus for the development of AI, often being labelled, alongside Zhongguancun in Beijing, as 'China's Silicon Valley' (e.g. Deng 2021). Indeed, Shenzhen may offer a more direct resemblance to the famous region of northern California, due to its rapid growth from the early 1980s. While Zhongguancun may be the spiritual home of China's technology industry, Shenzhen is surely symbolic of the post-1980s reform, and the meteoric urbanisation that underpins the current capacity for AI development. As Lee contends, it is in the production of hardware related to AI that Shenzhen has become particularly well known, as a 'go-to city for entrepreneurs who want to build new drones, robots, wearables, or intelligent machines' (Lee 2018, p125). As discussed above, it is also home to one of China's elite 'double first class' universities (specifically the Southern University of Science and Technology), and the site of one of only eight new 'AI innovation zones'.

AI and the revitalisation of the countryside

While Shenzhen is often hailed as a success story, not only of the SEZs, but also of the more contemporary focus on urban zones of technology innovation and AI specialisation, rural areas remain a key focus of government policy, particularly so for education. Following the reforms under Deng Xiaoping, successive leaders also sought to publicise wide-ranging policy initiatives aimed at addressing inequalities between rural and urban China, as well as between western and eastern regions. For example, the 'Great Western Development Strategy' (西部大开发) launched by Jiang Zemin in 1999, the slogan of 'the new socialist countryside' (社会主义新农村建设) coined by Hu Jintao in 2006, and 'Rural Revitalisation' under Xi Jinping. It is important to acknowledge the importance attached to such initiatives, given that they impact roughly 40% of the Chinese population,[3] as well as the ways a wide range of governance issues in China are often animated by attempts to manage the countryside. As Wang (2020) notes, both inside and outside of China, assumptions of 'metronormativity' tend to overlook the significance of rural society. Crucially, education is frequently positioned as a core means of addressing a range of development barriers experienced by rural areas, including a lack of access to resources and opportunities. As Yue et al. contend, '[i]f one is to understand China's development path over the past 40 years, it is crucial that the policies, trends, and successes of rural education are documented and understood' (2018, p94). Li (2020) outlines four broad stages of policy reform focused on rural compulsory education in China, which, since 1978, has sought to devolve governance responsibilities to regions, develop the training and retention of teachers in less-developed areas, as well as allocate funding for resources and equipment (Li 2020). As Yue et al. suggest, the resulting growth of educational opportunity has been unprecedented:

> Due to China's sheer size – and its rapid pace of growth – we are confident that there has never been as large an expansion of education, in terms of sheer numbers, as China has experienced over the past 40 years ... Most of this increase was from students in rural areas.
>
> (Yue et al. 2018, p104)

However, substantial disparities remain. As is often claimed, these result from a lack of funding: 'China's spending patterns favor urban students and schools, especially due to the focus on universities' (Yue et al. 2018, p106). With research derived from the large-scale Rural Education Action Program (or REAP),[4] Rozelle and Hell (2020) further address the economic implications of this inequality, suggesting that while China's recent development has been fuelled by low-skilled labour, often from rural migrants, the desired transition to high-income status would require substantial health and education reforms in the countryside. Liu et al. (2009) also attest to the ways education is often positioned as the means through which China might transform its economy away from an industrialised phase of low-paid factory jobs. Perhaps unsurprisingly, technology interventions have frequently been proposed as the tools through which issues of rural educational inequality can be addressed. The *National Plan for Medium and Long-Term Education Reform and Development* in 2010, for example, states: '[m]ajor efforts shall be given to build information infrastructure in rural schools so that the gap of digitalization between cities and countryside can be bridged' (MEPRC 2010, p41).

It is within this challenging educational and developmental context that the relationships between AI and education in China can be better understood. Significantly, private education, which has substantially underpinned the development of AI for education, as discussed in Chapters 3 and 4, also contributed to the expansion of educational inequality. While private schools for English-language learning and exam preparation served the increasing diversity of society in the 1990s (see Kleinman et al. 2011), they were located predominantly in the urban centres of the eastern and southern coastal regions (Wang 2001). This had the effect of amplifying inequalities and regional differences, as private education fuelled economic development in the cities. In this way, private education contributed to the regional inequalities that would be the target of subsequent educational AI initiatives, one example of which will be discussed below. This is because 'solving' educational inequalities has emerged as a central feature of the development of AI for education, bolstered by a long-standing policy discourse that frames rural education as a legitimate target of intervention.

TAL's (discussed in Chapters 3 and 4) much publicised 'AI teacher' project offers a prime example. As Wang (2019) reports, this particular AI system was used to teach Mandarin Chinese to the Yi ethnic group, living in the rural area of Zhaojue County, Liangshan Yi Autonomous Prefecture in Sichuan Province – an area which has been 'a key target of the national effort for poverty alleviation' (Wang 2019, p10). While this ethnic group has its own language, Mandarin is suggested to be 'a tool and necessary condition for them to enter the mainstream society', contributing 'to the full development and progress of individuals, thus promoting the development of the Yi region' (Wang 2019, p4). The lack of Mandarin for these students, it is suggested, 'greatly hinders their learning of other subjects at school' (Wang 2019, p11). As the report further emphasises, the lack of bilingual ability in this region results in a substantial lack of teachers able to teach Mandarin in the local language. Hence, the 'AI teacher' was designed to relieve the teaching deficit. The system thus 'performs bilingual teaching of the Yi language and Mandarin' (Wang 2019, p5), by drawing on 'speech recognition, speech evaluation and other technologies' to 'intelligently evaluate and correct children's pronunciation in real time, helping them learn both Mandarin and the Yi language' (Wang 2019, p9). Due to the low-resource context, the report also indicates that the 'AI teacher' was 'cross platform' and did not require 'sophisticated hardware or network support' (Wang 2019, p23). The 'AI teacher' has been deployed in '252 preschool teaching points and 72 primary schools' (Wang 2019, p7) – where 'teaching points' refers to rural teaching situations that may not represent formal schools – and it engaged 70,462 students (ibid). Drawing on interview data with teachers as well as test scores from students, Wang's (2019) report includes a detailed evaluation of the project, indicating some perceived successes with the efficiency of Mandarin teaching. The report also emphasises the participatory role of local Yi teachers and students, who contributed both recommendations and audio recordings for the AI system, such that 'the programme closely adapted to the local conditions and the learning habits of the local children … instead of pushing foreign experience directly to the local children and teachers' (Wang 2019, p26). The particular significance of this example follows from the discussion of government regulation in the previous chapter, and the questions over TAL's withdrawal from the private after-school education market, and their embracing of the role of 'national champion' for smart education (Larsen 2019;). While deploying AI as a highly profitable product within a lucrative private education market may no longer be appropriate in the post-'double reduction' regulatory landscape in China, framing the technology as addressing long-established issues of inequality might seem more favourable. Other similar high-profile projects have been announced, such as a collaboration between TAL, New Oriental, and the Qingxi Yuanshan Charity Foundation, to supply AI educational resources to rural areas (Koolearn 2019). Supposedly impacting 300,000 students since its launch (Vandenberg 2020), the project draws on an AI system to link rural face-to-face teaching with an online broadcast from an urban school. Directly connecting urban and rural education therefore seems to be a palatable orientation for AI development currently, at least in terms of the initiatives that companies want to be seen to publicise.

However, the solving of engrained regional inequalities in China's education system through the application of AI appears as yet another imagined future, in which data-driven technology simply replaces the shortfall in teachers, and manages to raise attainment levels in ways that straightforwardly overturn socio-economic disparities. Such a vision disregards underlying structural dynamics, including substantial internal migration (as described in the account of the origins of Shenzhen's development above). As Kleinman et al. (2011) observe, this migration has been substantial: '[t]here were an estimated two million migrant laborers in 1980 and by 2006 the number had grown to 132 million' (Kleinman 2011, p14). This internal migration has impacted education directly:

> Urbanization has exaggerated regional differences in educational access. The movement of people from rural to urban areas within China in search of employment opportunities and higher wages is among the largest internal migrations in human history.
>
> (ChinaPower 2016)

This means that '[l]ess economically developed regions often suffer from the migration of qualified teachers to more developed parts of the country and lack adequate funds to hire and properly train instructors' (ChinaPower 2016). It is precisely towards addressing this scarcity of teachers that many AI technologies are being developed. As discussed in Chapters 3 and 4, Squirrel AI has been explicit about its business model of targeting both after-school markets and state schools in second- and third-tier cities, precisely due to the perception of a lack of quality teachers. This reveals some of the entangled relationships through which AI development overlaps with differing policy visions for education. On the one hand, AI seems poised to fill the substantial gap in teaching provision within rural areas, as well as solve significant educational inequalities that have burdened the Chinese government for decades. On the other, AI appears to gloss over the underlying relocation of skilled educational professionals to more pros-perous areas, and legitimise the idea of teachers migrating to better-paid employment in cities. As such, these future visions seem incompatible, and indicate part of a delicate balance the Chinese government is required to achieve between lifting rural populations out of poverty and also maintain-ing the countryside as a source of food production, a supply of unskilled labour, and a contemporary consumerist population (Wang 2020). Both AI and education therefore seem to be intertwined in broader political and economic quandaries over the role of students and workers in the grand visions of data-driven futures. As Wang suggests, '[a]lthough China harbors dreams of becoming an AI superpower, the question of the countryside will have to be resolved in order for China to garner enough knowledge workers' (2020, p24).

Concluding remarks

This chapter has outlined a range of visions for the geographical orientation of AI and its relationships with education. A central facet of the broader imaginary of AI is the origin story of China's technology sector in Zhong-guancun, located in Beijing's northwest Haidian district. Famed for its elec-tronics market, subsequent government-sponsored science and technology development, and a vibrant entrepreneurial community inspired by the suc-cesses of Silicon Valley in the US, the area has underlying historical and con-temporary ties to educational institutions and academies. These institutions are not only imagined as supplying start-up AI companies with fresh grad-uates, but they are also assumed to bolster technical research and develop-ment through collaborative partnerships. Another overlapping imaginary for the local context of AI development may therefore be the university, positioned as a powerful node in regional networks, and guided towards elite status by the national 'double first class' strategy. The contemporary envisioning of urban centres of AI innovation is also linked to the older strategy of 'SEZs' which allowed the early stages of China's market reforms to experiment with controlled regions of commercial development. The cur-rent imaginaries of 'zones' of intensive AI innovation and high-performing universities thus aligns with a long-standing focus on cities as the engine of China's developmentalist strategy, exacerbating a range of deep inequalities between urban and rural areas. Following recent stringent regulations on the private after-school tuition market (examined in Chapter 4), through which educational AI in China has grown, explicitly addressing rural ine-qualities through the application of data-driven technology appears to be an acceptable direction for the development of new projects and initiatives. Nevertheless, purporting to replace rural teachers with automated AI seems to situate such educational initiatives within long-standing dilemmas about the relationships between countryside populations and China's urban developmentalist agenda.

As a final reflection, despite some key examples of educational AI being directed towards under-resourced rural areas for the ambitious aims of raising attainment and socio-economic status, profound regional disparities remain. Furthermore, it seems likely that such inequalities will be amplified through the emphasis on urban centres of technology innovation. As Hine (2022) contends, the vast majority of members of the key networks and collaborations around AI are located in first-tier cities, while the bulk of recent national science foundation funding went to Beijing, Shanghai, Jiangsu, and Guangdong.[5] Furthermore, future visions of urban development in China appear to hail a new era of 'city regions', 'mega city regions', or 'super mega city regions' (Yeh and Chen 2020), involving the linking and merging of existing cities for the purposes of increased economic activity. As Scott describes, city regions are 'large spatially extended urbanized areas ... locationally anchored by one or more metropolitan centers ... spreading far outwards into diffuse hinterlands' (Scott 2019, p554). The key economic ideas underpinning the city region, centred around agglomeration, tend to be framed in terms of the ways urban concentration and geographical proximity tend to raise productivity, as well as flows and exchanges of knowledge between businesses (Taylor and Derudder 2016). In this sense, city regions imagine the local entrepreneurial intensity of places like Zhongguancun on a grand scale. Indeed, China has emerged as a significant national hub for city regions (Scott 2019; Yeh and Chen 2020), linked to the country's rapid economic acceleration in recent decades, and to substantial population growth and urban migration since the market-reform period. Announced in 2016, the 13th Five-Year Plan (2016–2020) identified 19 city regions as 'the national engines of future urbanisation and economic growth' (Yeh and Chen 2020, p640). A recent report indicates that 11 of these have been given formal approval to proceed (Economist 2021). The three principal city regions in China are (1) the Beijing-Tianjin region (also linked to cities in Hebei province), (2) the Shanghai-Nanjing-Hangzhou region (more broadly, this is sometimes referred to as the Yangtze River delta region), and the Guangzhou-Shenzhen-Hong Kong region (often framed within a wider Pearl River delta region). According to Yeh and Chen, these three regions 'occupy only 5% of the national land area but are inhabited by 24% of the population and contributed over 40% of the GDP of the national total in 2015' (2020, p637). As discussed above, these city regions are also the central focus of government funding for infrastructure, research, and elite universities, all strategically directed towards the production and dissemination of AI. Indeed, 'technology-intensive production and software development' (Yeh and Chen 2020, p642) is underscored as a key example of geographically clustered economic activity in China's city regions. As such, despite the formidable challenges presented by China's rural areas, urbanisation on a grand scale appears to be the dominant vision of AI development, in which education is subsumed as a producer of the requisite human capital.

Notes

1 Dong et al. further suggest that the name Zhongguancun (中关村) was proposed by Yuan Chen, 'a famous historian and educator' (2019, p1), deriving from the older name of 'Zhong guan er', referring to a eunuch burial ground in the area during the Qing dynasty.
2 Hauben (2010) claims that the frequent references to Qian Tianbai as the sender of the first email from China are in error. Indeed, Dong et al. (2019) repeat this widely held view in their history of Zhongguancun.
3 Rural populations have been in steady decline since a high of over 80% in the 1960s, see https://data.worldbank.org/indicator/SP.RUR.TOTL.ZS?locations=CN
4 See https://sccei.fsi.stanford.edu/reap/
5 See National Natural Science Foundation of China 2019 annual report: https://www.nsfc.gov.cn/english/site_1/pdf/NSFC%20Annual%20Report%202019.pdf

References

Au, B. (2020). Xi starts tour of southern China to mark 40th anniversary of Shenzhen special economic zone. *South China Morning Post.* 13 October. https://www.scmp.com/video/china/3105255/xi-starts-tour-southern-china-mark-40th-anniversary-shenzhen-special-economic
Baruzzi, S. (2021). AI innovation zones in China: Opportunities for foreign investors. *China Briefing.* 3 March. https://www.china-briefing.com/news/ai-innovation-zones-in-china-opportunities-for-foreign-investors/#:~:text=On%20February%2020%2C%202021%2C%20the, Shenzhen%2C%20and%20 Jinan%2DQingdao.
Brown, K. (2020). *China.* Cambridge: Polity Press.
Chen, W. (2020). How Zhongguancun became the innovation hub powering China's tech aspirations. *KrASIA.* 17 December. Available: https://kr-asia.com/how-zhongguancun-became-the-innovation-hub-powering-chinas-tech-aspirations
China Power Team. (2016). How Does Education in China Compare with Other Countries? *China Power.* 15 November. Updated 2 September 2021. Accessed 15 August 2022. https://chinapower.csis.org/education-in-china/
Deng, I. (2021). Shenzhen, China's silicon valley, plans to turbocharge local AI development with first-of-a-kind regulations *South China Morning Post.* 30 June. https://www.scmp.com/tech/policy/article/3139319/shenzhen-chinas-silicon-valley-plans-turbocharge-local-ai-development
Dong, X., Hu, Y., Yin, W., & Kuo, E. (2019). The history of Zhongguancun: Building a park and establishing a benchmark. In *Zhongguancun Model: Driving the Dual Engines of Science & Technology and Capital.* Singapore: Springer. https://doi.org/10.1007/978-981-13-2267-9_1
Du, J. (2018). Peking university to open new campus in Changping district. *China Daily.* http://www.chinadaily.com.cn/a/201811/12/WS5be94439a310eff3032882ae.html
Economist. (2019). China's silicon valley is transforming China, but not yet the world. 13 July 2019. https://www.economist.com/china/2019/07/11/chinas-silicon-valley-is-transforming-china-but-not-yet-the-world Accessed 16th September 2021

Gao, X., Song, W., & Peng, X. (2015). National innovation demonstration zones leading China's regional development. *Modern Economy*, 6, 1056–1063. doi: 10.4236/me.2015.610102.

Hauben, J. (2010). The story of China's first email link and how it got corrected. Speech given to the School of Global Journalism and Communications in Chongqing. 12 January. Available: https://www.informatik.kit.edu/downloads/ HaubenJay-ChongqingSpeech-12Jan2010.pdf

Hine, E. (2022). All ChinAI policy is local. *China AI Newsletter*. 15 August. https:// chinai.substack.com/p/chinai-193-all-chinai-policy-is-local?utm_source= substack&utm_medium=email

Ke, J. (2018). University drivers AI research forward. *Shine*. https://www.shine.cn/ news/metro/1801199208/

Kleinman, A., Yan, Y., Jun, J, Lee, S., Zhang, E., Tianshu, P., Fei, W., & Jinhua, G. (2011). *Deep China: The moral life of the person*. Berkley: The University of California Press.

Koolearn. (2019). Social responsibility. https://www.koolearn.hk/#/

Larsen, B.C. (2019). China's national AI team: The role of National AI open innovation platforms. In AI Policy and China: Realities of State-Led Development, G. Webster (Ed.). Stanford-New America Digichina Project Special Report No. 1. pp. 21–25. https://newamerica.org/documents/4353/DigiChina-AI-report-20191029.pdf

Lee, K-F. (2018). *AI superpowers: China, silicon valley, and the new world order*. New York: Houghton Mifflin Harcourt.

Li, J. (2020). Compulsory educational policies in rural China since 1978: A macro perspective. *Beijing International Review of Education*, 2(1), 159–164. https://doi. org/10.1163/25902539-00201012

Li, S. (2018). From 985 to world class 2.0: China's strategic move. *Inside Higher Ed*. 7 February. https://www.insidehighered.com/blogs/world-view/985-world-class-20-chinas-strategic-move

Lin, C. (2006). *The transformation of Chinese socialism*. Durham, NC: Duke University Press.

Liu, C., Zhang, L., Luo, R., Rozelle, S., Sharbono, B., & Shi, Y. (2009). Development challenges, tuition barriers, and high school education in China. *Asia Pacific Journal of Education*, 29(4), 503–520. https://doi.org/10.1080/02188790903312698

MEPRC [Ministry of Education of the People's Republic of China]. (2010). National plan for medium and long-term education reform and development. UNESCO Translation available: https://uil.unesco.org/i/doc/lifelong-learning/policies/ china-outline-of-chinas-national-plan-for-medium-and-long-term-educationreform-and-development-2010-2020.pdf

MEPRC [Ministry of Education of the People's Republic of China] (2018[JK1]). Education informatization 2.0 action plan [in Chinese] http://www.moe.gov.cn/ srcsite/A16/s3342/201804/t20180425_334188.html

MEPRC [Ministry of Education of the People's Republic of China]. (2022). Notice of the Ministry of Education, Ministry of Finance and National Development and Reform Commission on the announcement of the second round of "Double First-Class" universities and construction disciplines. http://www.moe.gov.cn/ srcsite/A22/s7065/202202/t20220211_598710.html

Peterson, D., Goode, K., & Gehlhaus, D. (2021). AI Education in China and the United States: A comparative assessment. CSET [Center for Security and

Emerging Technology] Issue Brief. September 2021. Available: https://cset.georgetown.edu/wp-content/uploads/CSET-AI-Education-in-China-and-the-United-States-1.pdf

Roberts, H., Cowls, J., Morley, J., Taddeo, M., Wang, V., & Floridi, L. (2021). The Chinese approach to artificial intelligence: An analysis of policy, ethics, and regulation. *AI & Society*, 36, 59–77. https://doi.org/10.1007/s00146-020-00992-2

Rozelle, S., & Hell, N. (2020). *Invisible China. How the urban-rural divide threatens China's rise.* Chicago, IL: University of Chicago Press

Scott, A.J. (2019). City-regions reconsidered. *Environment and Planning A: Economy and Space*, 51(3), 554–580. https://doi.org/10.1177/0308518X19831591

Slater, M. (2018). List of China high-tech zones. *China Checkup.* 12 July. https://www.chinacheckup.com/blog/china-high-tech-zones

Sullivan, L.R., & Liu-Sullivan, N.Y. (2015). *Historical dictionary of science and technology in modern China.* Lanham: Rowman & Littlefield.

Taylor, P., & Derudder, B. (2016). *World city network: A global urban analysis.* Abingdon: Routledge.

Vandenberg, L. (2020). EdTech in Rural China. *The Diplomat.* 1 December. https://thediplomat.com/2020/12/edtech-in-rural-china/

Vincent, J. (2017). Google opens Chinese AI lab, says 'science has no borders'. *The Verge.* 13 December. https://www.theverge.com/2017/12/13/16771134/google-ai-lab-china-research-center

Wang, P. (2001). Private education emerges in modern China: A comparative case study. *NUCB Journal of Language Culture and Communication*, 3(2), 105–115.

Wang, X. (2019). TAL "using AI language teaching system to innovate language learning of under-resourced students" programme. Report. https://aiteacher.100tal.com/file/TAL%20%E2%80%9CUsing%20AI%20Language%20Teaching%20System%20to%20Innovate%20Language%20Learning%20of%20Under-Resourced%20Students%E2%80%9D%20Programme%20Progressive%20Evaluation%20Report%EF%BC%881123%EF%BC%89.pdf

Wang, X. (2020). *Blockchain chicken farm, and other stories of tech in China's countryside.* New York: FSG Originals X Logic.

Yeh, A.G.-O., & Chen, Z. (2020). From cities to super mega city regions in China in a new wave of urbanisation and economic transition: Issues and challenges. *Urban Studies,* 57(3), 636–654. https://doi.org/10.1177/0042098019879566

Yue, A., Tang, B., Shi, Y., Tang, J., Shang, G., Medina, A., & Rozelle, S. (2018). Rural education across China's 40 years of reform: Past successes and future challenges. *China Agricultural Economic Review*, 10(1), 93–118. https://doi.org/10.1108/CAER-11-2017-0222

6 'Talent' and the international flow of AI expertise

This chapter examines notions of artificial intelligence (AI) expertise, frequently referred to as 'AI talent', as another prominent dimension of the sociotechnical imaginary of data-driven technology emerging in China. Here, skills in related computer science techniques, bestowed on students through various educational routes, are assumed to provide the requisite human capital for the broader vision of geopolitical AI ascendency and national economic transformation, as examined principally in Chapter 2. As will be detailed below, central to this narrative of AI futures, propagated not just in China but also in the US, is the idea of an educational 'pipeline', through which students, at an increasingly young age, are imagined to be funnelled into high-level research, and ultimately the data-driven economy.

However, while this largely domestic vision for training in AI skills assumes an education system tightly coupled with business demands in the technology sector, the notion of 'talent' will be suggested in the second part of the chapter to have a longer history, particularly through China's efforts to address waves of emigration following the 'opening up reforms of the late 1970s'. 'Talent' thus also refers to significant populations of Chinese scientists and scholars who are now envisioned as experts who can be enticed back to China, principally from positions in the US, in the name of serving a nationalist and developmentalist agenda around AI. The extent to which there is an 'international' dimension to China's AI, as will be the concern of the subsequent discussion, therefore involves an examination of broader flows of expertise, as Chinese nationals travel for study and migrate for work. Such a focus on 'expertise', and its movement across nations, ultimately diverts attention from any sense of 'national AI capacity' (as discussed previously in Chapter 2), and begins to signal a wider frame of reference through which AI development might be understood. Looking further back, this chapter will also discuss early 20th-century ties between China and the US, and a significant tradition of Chinese scholars seeking out technical knowledge across the Pacific for their own country's modernisation.

The final part of the chapter will examine a proliferating area of research which is focused on analysing, measuring, quantifying, and comparing

DOI: 10.4324/9781003375135-6

'national capacity' in AI. This is often concerned, not only with the extent to which national education systems are geared to supply a future data-driven economy with skilled labour, but also with tracking, in minute detail, the migratory flow of graduates, postgraduates, and postdoctoral researchers, with the intention of identifying shifting trends. In this way, researching 'national AI capacity' contributes to the imaginary of AI as a means for geo-political positioning, in which narrow statistical measures are used to rank nation states and institutions according to their presumed ability to harness data-driven technologies for developmental means.

Cultivating Chinese AI 'talent'

One of the key government policies outlining strategic plans for the rela-tionships between AI and education, the *Action Plan for Artificial Intelli-gence Innovation in Colleges and Universities*, or APAICU (also discussed in Chapter 2), foregrounds 'discipline development and talent training' (MEPRC 2018a). This refers to the two central aspects of government strat-egy of AI education, which are focused most prominently on higher educa-tion: first, the defining of a specific curriculum for teaching AI techniques, alongside the implementation of courses of study; and, second, the training of new generations of 'talented' students with the requisite technical skills and understanding. This is the basis of the government drive to instil AI training within the formal education system, and link such learning directly to the burgeoning technology industry, for the purposes of driving the sup-posed data-driven economy.

The APAICU is explicit about the need for new fields of learning focused on AI, calling for the support of 'colleges and universities to set up artifi-cial intelligence disciplines in computer science and technology disciplines' (MEPRC 2018a). The policy further emphasises the need to 'promote the construction of first-level disciplines in the field of artificial intelligence' (MEPRC 2018a). Here 'first-level disciplines' refers to nationally recognised standards for the delivery of a particular disciplinary subject at the univer-sity level, which can be awarded to particular institutions where criteria are met. This would thus align any new 'AI discipline' with the established structures for subject provision in higher education China. Relatedly, the APAICU also suggests: 'increase investment in related disciplines in the field of artificial intelligence in the construction of "double first-class"' (MEPRC 2018a), referring to the new system of university ranking intro-duced in 2015 (as also discussed in the previous chapter). 'Double first-class' is a term used to describe elite universities in China which are designated as 'world first-class' institutions, as well as developing 'first-level disciplines'. In this sense, the development of AI as a subject discipline is being aligned with one of the key policy initiatives in higher education in China, focused specifically on building high-ranking Chinese universities into world-leading institutions (see State Council 2015). Peterson et al. (2021) suggest the 'Double first-class' initiative as one of the foundations for developing AI training, allowing the government to focus on the reform of China's elite universities.

Alongside the development of a specific subject discipline in AI, the APA-ICU also calls for interdisciplinary links across other areas of higher education, encouraging '[t]he cross-integration of education, physics, biology, psychology, sociology, law and other disciplines and professional education, to explore the 'artificial intelligence + X' talent training model (MEPRC 2018a). Here, technical skills associated with AI are positioned as amenable to combination with other university disciplines, presumably under the assumption that such areas will be enhanced and 'future-proofed' as a result. Further, the 'artificial intelligence + X' plans seem concerned with expanding the training of AI skills beyond the boundaries of computer science departments, so that no area of the university is without an opportunity to develop technical capacity in data-driven innovation as discussed in Chapters 3 and 4. This appears to underscore the idea of broad reform brought about by the development of AI, not just as a particular set of techniques within the technical discipline of computer science, but as a transformational method, able to enhance and augment other aspects of the university, and, ultimately, the industries and professions to which graduates will be headed.

By March 2021, 345 educational institutions were approved to offer degrees majoring in AI (Peterson et al. 2021), making it the most popular new major in China for two years consecutively (Zou 2021). Additionally, analyses of Baidu search results indicate that AI is the most searched degree major in China in 2022, and has been ranked first for three consecutive years (Wang 2022), suggesting that the curriculum development encouraged by government policy is translating into substantial interest from new students. As Peterson et al.'s (2021) research shows, AI majors are distributed across China, principally in the eastern, central, and southern provinces, reflecting the geographical divides discussed in Chapter 5. A report from the Australian government's Department of Education, Skills, and Employment confirms this disparity, suggesting:

> the majority of disciplines to be developed are still clustered in major cosmopolitan areas in the eastern region of China. Beijing topped the chart with 162 disciplines, followed by Shanghai with 57 and Jiangsu with 43. These three provinces together have more than half of the total disciplines to be developed.
>
> (DESE 2017)

Peterson et al. (2021) also emphasise the links between these majors and AI research institutes, which reveals a strong association in all of the eastern coastal provinces, as discussed in the previous chapter.

The APAICU appears to emphasise that teacher training is a key aspect of delivering the ambitions plans for AI education. The policy suggests:

> Accelerate the transformation of scientific and technological achievements and resources in the field of artificial intelligence into education and teaching, and promote the construction of teaching materials and online open courses in important directions of artificial intelligence, especially the foundation of artificial intelligence, machine learning, neural networks, pattern recognition, computer vision, knowledge engineering, and natural language processing.
>
> (MEPRC 2018a)

Such development therefore appears to involve direct links between the latest research and development outcomes and the production of learning materials, suggesting a greater need for universities to disseminate the work of their AI laboratories. The policy also encourages a 'universal education', involving the establishment of 'a public service platform for artificial intelligence science popularization for young people and the general public' (MEPRC 2018a). It also suggests '[a]rtificial intelligence-related knowledge and skill courses should be set up in training and on-the-job training' and 'courses should be set up in non-academic continuing education training in colleges and universities' (MEPRC 2018a). This implies, not just a revision of teaching in formal education to incorporate AI skills, but a broader approach to extend such training to other forms of informal, adult, and continuing education. However, it is perhaps the clear emphasis on links with industry that is most significant in the APAICU, implying that the value of AI training cannot be derived exclusively from the work undertaken in university research laboratories. The APAICU suggests:

> Deepen industry-university cooperation and collaborative education, promote the implementation of industry-university cooperation and collaborative education projects in the field of artificial intelligence, and promote talent training reforms with the latest achievements in industrial and technological development.
>
> (MEPRC 2018a).

While, as discussed in Chapter 2, universities are positioned as core sites of development for AI, here the APAICU acknowledges the key role of industry in shaping the vision for skills development. AI laboratories may well excel in developing specific data-driven techniques; however, it seems clear that education and training in such skills cannot serve a wider purpose without insights from businesses, and the sense in which knowledge of AI can be put to use in the economy. Furthermore, the formal role of industry implies a distinct orientation towards the vocationalisation of higher education in

China, where businesses are able to shape the learning outcomes of students, and the ultimate goal of the university experience is framed in terms of viable employment. Indeed, where government policy appears to envision a future economic revolution underpinned by AI technology, such promises are ultimately contingent upon a newly skilled workforce, and an education system to produce it. The government interest in vocational education is apparent in recent revisions to the *Vocational Education Law*, first introduced in 1996 and subsequently updated in the spring of 2022 (see MEPRC 2022). According to Koty (2022), these revisions are aimed at raising the status of vocational education, which has traditionally been reserved for those with lower exam scores, in order to meet the demands of a shifting manufacturing landscape that requires skilled labour. While the *Vocational Education Law* doesn't refer to AI specifically, the recent adjustments demonstrate that the Chinese government is keenly focused on the relationships between education and industry, and is willing to undertake reforms in service of a developmentalist agenda. The creation of an AI subject discipline may be envisaged for general, rather than vocational, education, but the links to industry involvement in the scoping and development of such a curriculum are nevertheless explicit in the APAICU, and the omnipresent references to 'talent' underscore the assumption of formal links to employable technical skills. Nevertheless, some specific collaborations with industry appear to be bridging the gap between general and vocational education. An initiative launched in July 2019 by Baidu, in collaboration with Beijing Changping Vocational School, established a 'vocational school-enterprise cooperation initiative on AI education' (Peterson et al. 2021, p12), suggesting the development of both vocational courses on applied AI and teacher-training programmes. This indicates that the private sector may view vocational education as a better source of skilled workers than graduates of general education, who are typically required to undertake broader programmes of study.

One of the key areas of industry collaboration is through formal partnerships with universities, principally through the Information Technology New Engineering Industry-University-Research Alliance (信息技术 新工科产学研联盟), comprising key government bodies (the Ministries of Education and Industry and Information Technology), universities (all of China's elite 'C9 league' institutions), and private companies (including Chinese tech giants Baidu, Alibaba, Tencent, Huawei, and China Telecom, but also US firms Cisco, IBM, and Microsoft) (Peterson et al. 2021). Peterson et al. (2021) suggest Baidu as a particularly important example of private sector collaboration, the company having established nine partnerships with universities in recent years for a range of activities focusing on developing AI curricula and resources, as well as training teachers. Another important area of collaboration is in the production of textbooks, which serve as an encapsulation of standardised and authoritative knowledge about AI for a given education level. This involvement provides the private sector with the ability to directly shape the content and direction of training in AI, and ultimately the form of expertise emerging from education and entering the workforce. Notable examples tend to be directed at high-school-level education, including *Fundamentals of Artificial Intelligence*, published in April 2018 by Sensetime (discussed in Chapter 3) in collaboration with East China Normal University (Sensetime 2022). The textbook was piloted in over 100 Chinese schools across five provinces, as well as Beijing and Shanghai, with Sensetime providing dedicated training to over 900 teachers to enable them to deliver the content (Liu 2019). Later in the same year, *Artificial Intelligence Experiment Materials* was published through a collaboration between the Institute of Automation of the Chinese Academy of Sciences and Google, attracting considerable attention for aiming some of the content towards pre-school levels (Peng 2018). The 33-volume textbook was in fact designed to cover a range of levels from pre-school to high school, as well as including material aimed at training teachers. Also significant in this initiative is the inclusion of a cloud-based learning platform, developed by Google AI in Beijing, providing students with access to programming environments and machine learning frameworks (Peng 2018). Additionally, in November 2018, a company backed by Tencent, UBTech Robotics, co-published *Future Intelligent Creator on AI-Series of Artificial Intelligence Excellent Courses for Primary and Secondary Schools* with East China Normal University (Peterson et al. 2021). While these examples demonstrate the ways the private sector is directly shaping AI training, it is clear that academia remains a key influence, with East China Normal University emerging as a central player. Indeed, the announcement in early 2020 that Professor Yao Qizhi, Dean of the Institute of Interdisciplinary Information at Tsinghua University and the first Chinese Turing Award winner, would be editing an AI textbook for high-school students attracted considerable attention (Sohu 2020; Peterson et al. 2021), attesting, perhaps, to the assumption of authoritative knowledge within the university.

While the development of an AI curriculum is a key focus of China's strategy, the production of 'talent' also appears to be a key term, often used to make explicit references to the training of a newly skilled workforce. The central three-step aims of the APAICU policy (also examined in Chapter 2) include specific references to 'talent', underscoring its central importance to the wider plans for AI development: by 2020, 'the advantages of talent training … will be further improved'; by 2025 'colleges and universities will have significantly improved … the quality of talent training'; and by 2030, there will be a 'talent guarantee' for China 'to become the forefront of innovative countries' (MEPRC 2018a). Mirroring the ambitions of the more widely publicised National Strategy for AI Development (or NSAID, discussed in Chapter 2), these aims underscore the central importance of education in the broader plans for geopolitical dominance in the field of data-driven technology, through the central theme of the 'talented' graduate. The 'colleges and universities' of the policy's title are framed here as the core producers of AI expertise, and the future workforce required to elevate China's position internationally. This nationalist component is emphasised further across the policy, suggesting for example, 'through the cultivation of innovative talents, we will continuously improve the national independent innovation level and build the advantages of continuous innovation and development' (MEPRC 2018a). A substantial burden of responsibility, therefore, appears to be placed upon the generation of 'talent', which has to not only instil high-level technical skills and expertise across the population, but also bolster the sense of national development, and secure China's place at the forefront of geopolitical rivalries over AI. 'Talent' is also a key term in other policy, for example, the *Education Informatization 2.0 Action Plan* (also examined further in Chapter 2). Aspects of this policy make clear the links between the perception of technological change and the need for education reform to produce newly skilled kinds of workers: '[t]he rapid development of artificial intelligence, big data, blockchain and other technologies will profoundly change the demand for talents and the form of education' (MEPRC 2018b). Calls for momentous change are also conveyed through statements such as '[s]tanding at a new historical starting point, we must focus on the new needs for talent training in the new era' (MEPRC 2018b). While 'talent' generally refers to technical training across all educational levels, it is graduate education that has been given substantial attention in terms of its potential to produce high-level expertise in AI. Peterson et al. note that doctoral training has been significantly reformed with increased funding, and the aim of generating 'a revolving door between industry and universities' (2021, p20). Through such plans, AI companies are encouraged to not only train university teachers in the latest techniques, but also provide data, case studies, and training platforms to graduate students. In return, company employees are granted access to universities in order to conduct research, often at recently formed AI institutes which, as of 2021, have been established at 34 universities in China (Peterson et al. 2021).

With such ambitious plans, not only to transform general education into the near-ubiquitous teaching and learning of AI techniques, but also to align such practices with industry in an overt attempt to drive the economy, it is perhaps not surprising that think tanks and policy analysts elsewhere have taken notice. Peterson et al.'s (2021) report (referenced above) was produced by the Centre for Security and Emerging Technology (CSET), a think tank based at Georgetown University in Washington DC, and makes a direct comparison between the AI education strategies of China and the US, with the explicit aim of recommending ways in which the latter might retain global competitiveness. The report centres on China's 'centralized authority' as the key difference between the two national strategies, whereas the approach of the US is described as 'piecemeal' in comparison (Peterson et al. 2021, p1). While the report examines the benefits and drawbacks of both contexts, it is perhaps most significant in its emphasis on guidance for future US strategy:

> to effectively face the competition presented by China for AI leadership, the United States needs to address some of the challenges inherent with its decentralized system and approach. We also suggest future US S&T [science and technology] education and workforce policy should be considered in a globally competitive context, instead of viewing it myopically as a domestic challenge.
>
> (Peterson et al. 2021, p39)

This seems to demonstrate the ways in which China's assertive policy-making around the development of AI training is being taken rather seriously in the US, and, arguably, used to justify a similar, all-encompassing strategy, in which the education system is transformed to serve the imaginary of the future data-driven economy. Here, any individual or societal goals and purposes for education appear to be rendered subservient to the needs of global economic competition. While Peterson et al.'s conclusions emphasise the potential strengths of China's broad policy strategy for AI education, there is little to challenge the instrumental view of education as a tool for workforce production:

> China's efforts to increase AI education at all levels bears important implications. Standardized curricula, centralized plans for implementing AI education, and explicitly calling upon companies to help universities all grant China higher likelihood of developing a robust talent pipeline for solving AI challenges.
>
> (Peterson et al. 2021, p38)

Education thus appears to be reduced to a 'talent pipeline' for government strategy, and reformed to serve the nationalist and developmentalist agenda for geopolitical dominance in the field of AI. Indeed, leaving such assumptions unchallenged, and portraying Chinese educational policy in terms of a unified and coherent route to AI ascendency, appears to provide an apt justification for similar reforms elsewhere. In a subsequent media article, two of the CSET report's authors contend: 'China is actively integrating AI into every level of its education system, while the United States has yet to embrace AI education as a strategic priority. This will not do' (Goode and Peterson 2022). The reform of education to embrace training in AI skills therefore seems to be thoroughly embroiled in the wider geopolitical tensions between the US and China, where the threat of new generations of foreign 'talent' can be used as a vindication for sweeping domestic reforms that privilege international competitiveness, and position educational endeavours as subservient to nationalist agendas and economic strategising.

However, the notion of 'talent' has much broader connotations than exclusively the training of students through the education system. As the next section will examine, 'talent' is also used to refer to existing technical expertise, and, as such, it opens up wider possibilities for understanding the transnational dimensions of expert AI knowledge.

International flows of 'AI talent'

The prominence of the notion of 'talent' in Chinese discourse did not originate, of course, with the recent policy-making around AI. As Jia (2018) details, for example, the central government launched a major 'Thousand Talents' (千人计划) programme in 2008, specifically devised to entice 'leading Chinese scientists, academics and entrepreneurs living abroad back to China' (2018, p8). The project was updated in 2011 to include foreign experts rather than Chinese nationals exclusively, and by 2018 had attracted over 7,000 people to work in China (Jia 2018). Thus, the aim of the initiative was 'to target professors and chief scientists in the West', who, if persuaded to return to scientific, academic, or entrepreneurial careers in China, would 'gain access to much higher salaries and research funding levels than their locally trained peers' (Jia 2018, p8). The significance of the 'Thousand Talents' programme is in its explicit acknowledgement of the long-standing emigration of particular kinds of expertise from China, and the sense in which 'talent' infers, not just expertise that is 'homegrown' through the Chinese education system, but also educational and professional experience that has been honed in more developed academic and scientific communities, principally in the US. Indeed, as Cao examines, China experienced a substantial 'brain drain' between 1978 and 2007, when 'more than 1.21 million Chinese went abroad for study and research, of whom only about a quarter have returned' (2008, p331). By some estimates the Chinese diaspora of scientists and scholars is over 400,000 (Schiermeier 2014), suggesting a substantial pool of candidates that might be persuaded to return to China. In this sense, the Chinese government's interest in 'talent' is not exclusively focused on reforming its own internal education system to produce the requisite skills, but is also concerned with influencing international flows of expertise to ensure that China's workforce is suitably populated. As will be detailed in this section, expertise in AI is now a key focus of this external view of 'talent'. Indeed, this is made explicit in the State Council's *New Generation Artificial Intelligence Development Plan*, which calls for the 'Thousand Talents' programme to be utilised as a key mechanism to attract AI expertise back to China. As such, just like the wider 'Thousand Talents' initiatives which have been accused by the US government of explicitly seeking to gain access to new technologies for strategic advantage (Wray 2020), the transnational trajectories of AI expertise have become entangled in broader geopolitical contestations. The programme has generated some high-profile examples of returning 'talent', including the aforementioned Turing Award winner Professor QiZhi Yao, who, previous to his involvement in AI text-books, renounced his US citizenship to take up his current position at Tsin-ghua University in Beijing (Ding 2018). Furthermore, specific to the AI era of talent recruitment, the private sector has become substantially involved, principally through setting up overseas research centres and institutes in order to recruit experts into employment at Chinese technology companies (Ding 2018). Importantly, this demonstrates another key dimension of the private sector's central role in China's AI strategy, and also the distributed, rather than 'top down' avenues through which it operates (Ding 2018). Ding (2018) notes additional high-profile examples in this aspect of talent recruit-ment, including Andrew Ng, who had previously worked as chief of Google Brain, and subsequently took up a position at Baidu for three years, and Qi Lu, formerly executive vice president of Microsoft, and now Baidu's Chief Operating Officer. While the return of businesspeople and entrepreneurs has been relatively successful, the 'Thousand Talents' programme has been criticised for its apparent failure to persuade high-level academic experts to return to China permanently, particularly those with a PhD from the US (Sharma 2013).

Underpinning latest schemes to influence overseas 'talent', there is a rich history to Chinese citizens studying abroad. Wang (2002) examines the early 20th-century reform period as a particularly notable time for science educa-tion, where Chinese students were driven by ideas of using such knowledge to transform and modernise China. As Ye describes, an imperial decree by the Qing government in 1908 authorised the interest in scientific knowl-edge, declaring 'that all government students should study such subjects as engineering, agriculture, and natural sciences' (2001, p53). Subsequently, the Boxer Indemnity Scholarships, established in 1909 to support Chinese students to travel to the US, became a key vehicle for training in techni-cal subjects, requiring Chinese recipients to focus 80% of their studies on practical scientific knowledge (Ye 2001). As Ye (2001) further discusses, this turn to scientific learning was not only directly linked to the sense of humil-iation suffered after China's defeat in the first Sino-Japanese war (as dis-cussed previously in Chapter 2), but also widely interpreted as involving the acquisition of purely technical knowledge. As such, the attempts to develop 'Western' scientific knowledge during this time 'actually sustained and even enhanced the pragmatic strand in Chinese thinking' (Ye 2001, p54) which derived from Confucian tradition. In other words, rather than a break from the past, the focus on engineering, agriculture, and the natural sciences in this period was approached with a sense of continuity, where practical sci-ence was viewed as a means to serve the agenda of national development. The contemporary government strategy to gather AI expertise might there-fore be understood as an extension of a long-standing endeavour to acquire knowledge from abroad for the purposes of modernisation. That the US was the key destination for early 20th-century Chinese scholars, as it arguably is today for the development of AI expertise (see further below), provides an additional sense of continuity, as well as a testament to the close ties, as opposed to rivalries, that exist between the two countries. As Ye emphasises, '[t]o many Chinese students in America at the turn of the century, modernization was essentially the same thing as industrialisation, and America was seen as the model' (Ye 2001, p55), and it was industrialisation that was the ultimate goal of the attempts to foster learning engineering, agriculture, and the natural sciences.

Wang (2002) also details the formation of the first Chinese scientific association, the Science Society of China, which was established by a group of Boxer Indemnity Scholarship students at Cornell University in 1914. As Wang (2002) contends, this group was an important example of the sentiments at the time, in which such students were driven by a profound sense of duty to return to China and use their newly acquired knowledge to build a modern nation. From this viewpoint, the contemporary plans to entice 'talent' back to China presents an entirely different scenario, as many Chinese nationals with foreign qualifications and academic positions appear reluctant to do so. Nevertheless, Cao (2008) posits that the emphasis on overseas training was maintained after the establishment of the People's Republic of China (PRC) in 1949, where 'China did not experience a shortage of high-quality personnel for its economic, educational and scientific enterprises' (2008, p332). While the Cultural Revolution (1966–1976) all but brought about an end to studying abroad, it was revived after 1978, during the 'reform and opening up' (改革开放) period under Deng Xiaoping. For Cao, this marked a new period of unparalleled international study:

> This wave of Chinese nationals embarking on overseas study is historically unprecedented not only in terms of the number of students who have gone overseas, but also the number of returnees (319,700) which alone exceeds the total number of Chinese who studied abroad between 1847 and 1978.
>
> (Cao 2008, p332)

While the subjects studied after the late 1970s reforms were much broader than the specific practical science emphasised at the turn of the century, Deng emphasised the need for overseas study as a key way to develop both domestic education and science (Cao 2008). As such, learning from foreign countries was still framed as a fundamentally nationalist and developmentalist project, where travel to foreign institutions was portrayed in terms of priorities for the state, rather than those of the individual. Nevertheless, centralised control was further reduced in 1981 when self-sponsored overseas study was permitted (Cao 2008). Questions about the negative consequences of opening up remained, principally due to the growing realisation that many who travelled abroad for study never returned to China. As Cao (2008) notes, Zhao Zhiyang, general secretary of the CCP (Chinese Communist Party) Central Committee at the time, argued in 1987 that the reported 'brain drain' was in fact 'storing brainpower overseas' (Zweig and Chen 1995) so that it could eventually be utilised. One might therefore see the 'Thousand Talents' programme, and others like it, as attempting to restore this outlying supply of expertise, which in current times is focused on skills and knowledge related to AI.

Cao refers to two key subsequent events – the Tiananmen Square protests in 1989 and the changing of US policy in 1992 to allow Chinese nationals to remain in the country and seek residential status – as key factors in 'the first large unexpected "exodus" of highly qualified Chinese students who were supposed to return to China to shoulder the important historical responsibility of contributing to its modernisation drive' (Cao 2008, p333). Despite some initially negative reactions from the Chinese government to this mass departure of expertise, the situation was largely accepted by the turn of the century, particularly when Jiang Zemin, then CCP Central Committee General Secretary, publicised an acknowledgement (Cao 2008). Thus, maintains Cao, Chinese students:

> remaining overseas in universities, research laboratories and corporations is not an indication that China would lose them completely and permanently; quite on the contrary, they are among China's greatest assets, from which the nation may benefit in the long run.
>
> (Cao 2008, p334)

As such, China's significant immigrant population of AI 'talent', many of whom have trained and worked in the US, appears to be imagined by the Chinese government as permanently reachable, and always part of a reserve of expertise that will eventually contribute to national priorities.

Tracking 'AI talent'

In recent years, a significant area of research has emerged around an apparent aim of measuring 'AI capacity', often with an explicit agenda of comparing the US and China, and frequently with a particular focus on education as a contributing factor. In an important sense, this research surfaces as another kind of AI imaginary, not only where various aspects of technical development can be quantified at the national level and ranked internationally, but also where such measures begin to instil standards for acceptable kinds of strategy, often involving very particular criteria and specifications for education. In other words, such 'AI indexes', while purporting to objectively assess technical capacity, end up establishing the norms to which subsequent strategies will gravitate. As will be examined below, this has substantial implications for education, particularly where research outputs and institutional functions are rendered through narrow statistical calculations, and universities are increasingly positioned as suppliers of 'AI talent' defined by an imagined data-driven economy.

A number of high-profile reports focusing on 'indexing' 'national AI' have been published in recent years, including the *Government AI Readiness Index* (Nettel et al. 2021), the *Artificial Intelligence Index Report* (Zhang et al. 2022), the *Global AI Index* (Tortois 2022), and the *IBM Global AI Adoption Index* (IBM 2022). The extent to which education features in these studies is potentially revealing about the perceived importance of schools and universities in the broader visions of AI strategy, as well as the populations of 'talent' supposedly channelled into productive 'pipelines' for economic activity. The *Government AI Readiness Index* (Nettel et al. 2021) only includes the 'education level' of individuals as a variable within a measure of 'human capital', a subtheme of the 'Technology Sector'. Despite acknowledging the centrality of educational reform in many national AI policies, the 'readiness index' does not appear to include any formal analysis of education strategy. The *IBM Global AI Adoption Index* is focused principally on the private sector, rather than government policy. Hence, while the report specifies '[l]imited AI skills, expertise or knowledge' as one of the principal 'barriers' to AI adoption amongst private companies, there is no further mention of the role of formal education. The *Global AI Index* includes two measures of the number of universities in a given country offering AI-related postgraduate education, within the broader theme of 'research' (Tortois 2022). However, there appears to be no consideration of national educational strategy, or undergraduate and school-level curricula related to AI. Nevertheless, the *Global AI Index* features 'talent' as one of seven factors in their national ranking of AI, 'to benchmark nations on their level of investment, innovation and implementation' (Tortois 2022). Interestingly, while China is ranked second overall, behind the US, they are positioned only 24th for 'talent'. The calculation of the 'talent' score is derived from analysing indications of nationality from online profiles in various online platforms for the tech community, such as LinkedIn, Google Stack Overflow, and GitHub.

The *Artificial Intelligence Index Report* (Zhang et al. 2022) provides the most detailed information compared to the reports outlined above, in terms of PhD graduation rates and topics in AI subfields; however, the data is focused only on North America and the US. However, the measure of international students studying PhDs in the US provides some key insight, suggesting 'among the new AI PhDs from 2010 to 2020 who are US residents, the largest percentage has been non-Hispanic white and Asian – 65.2% and 18.8% on average' (Zhang et al. 2022). In 2020 there were 50.86% White (non-Hispanic) and 30.17% Asian PhD students. While the 'Asian' category is not broken down further into nationality, this suggests a strong contribution from Chinese nationals to AI research in the US.

Ranking institutions according to publications in AI-related disciplines is another prominent area of research, often concluding that Chinese universities may be benefiting from the strategic focus on 'talent'. According to Berger's (2021) analysis, between 2012 and 2017 (the year China's central AI strategy policy was announced), the top ten institutions for AI publications feature five US universities, with Carnegie Mellon University occupying first place. In this period, three Chinese institutions are in the top ten: Tsinghua University, Peking University, and the Chinese Academy of Sciences, occupying the second, third, and seventh places, respectively (ibid). Between 2017 and 2022, the ranking shifts considerably, with five Chinese institutions in the top ten. Tsinghua University and Peking University occupy the first and second places, respectively, and are joined by the Chinese Academy of Sciences in fourth, Zhejiang University in fifth, and Shanghai Jiao Tong University in eighth (ibid). Only three US institutions remain in the top ten, Carnegie Mellon University in third, University of Illinois at Urbana-Champaign in fifth (tied with Shanghai Jiao Tong above), and Cornell University dropping to ninth (ibid).

How much significance one might attribute to such statistical measures is difficult to discern. First, the separation between Berger's (2021) categories of 'AI' into, for example, 'Theory' (which includes 'algorithms and complexity') and 'Interdisciplinary areas' (which includes 'Robotics') calls into question the boundaries between 'AI' and other areas of computer science. Indeed, with just these two other sub-categories included in the analysis, the rankings change rather dramatically: Carnegie Mellon University holds the top spot in both date ranges, and only Tsinghua University makes it into the top ten (ranked fifth) between 2014 and 2017. Between 2017 and 2022 Tsinghua University (second) and Peking University (third) are China's only institutions in the top ten. Second, ranking exclusively according to number of publications only provides, arguably, a narrow measure of a university's research capacity, overlooking not only the quality of the publication output, but also other kinds of research outputs, impact and knowledge exchange activities, and collaborations that departments are presumably involved in.

It is also notable in Berger's (2021) analysis that while Tsinghua University and Peking University rank first and second for all 'AI' categories (2017–2022), their outputs in 'AI Theory' are very low (10 and 11, respectively) compared with third placed Carnegie Mellon University (with 155). This may reflect an overall neglect of theoretical perspectives in favour of straightforward development and practical application, which would align with the developmentalist approach incentivised by government policy. Furthermore, it may indicate deeper links to China's engagement with Western technical knowledge in the early 20th century, which, as discussed above, tended to focus on practical applications, rather than underlying theoretical insights. Liu appears to confirm this, suggesting, '[c]ompared to other countries, Chinese research into AI focuses more on practical applications rather than fundamental research' (Liu 2021). However, Liu (ibid) suggests this picture might be changing, as more references to fundamental research are beginning to appear in publications from China.

Other similar analyses of publications in AI-related fields claim 'Chinese universities and industry labs are still not publishing "best-in-class" research at the top AI conferences, where US institutions are the clear leaders' (Maro Polo 2022a). This is claimed through an analysis of the numbers of papers accepted for oral presentation at the *Conference and Workshop on Neural Information Processing Systems* (one of the most prestigious and highly selective 'AI' conferences, known as NeurIPS, and formerly as NIPS) in 2017, which indicated that 128 authors were affiliated with the US, while only 2 were affiliated with China (MarcoPolo 2022a). However, while this focus on NeurIPS as a measure of 'top-tier' research might sharpen the comparison between Chinese and US institutions, it also substantially narrows the view of AI development more generally, and overlooks the contributions of many other faculty members who, for example, may be involved in applying and disseminating knowledge and practice in the field, and thus raising the profile of the institution in other ways. Furthermore, such statistics are focused on individual institutions as well as their individual researchers as is the case with Berger's (2021) analysis, and the intention to establish a national comparison is implicit.

However, perhaps most significantly for the interest in 'talent' in this chapter, an examination of the country in which these authors undertook their undergraduate degrees (from which one can presumably infer nationality) reveals a substantial proportion from China – 25, as opposed to 50 from the US (MarcoPolo 2022a). In other words, of the 128 authors with an affiliation to the US, a substantial proportion of these are Chinese nationals who have immigrated for study and/or work in the area of AI. This demonstrates the inadequacy of a purely national framing for AI expertise, and points, not only to a substantial international dimension to the development of such 'talent', but also to, arguably, a specific and highly productive relationship between China and the US. Further research of AI 'talent' from the 2019 NeurIPS conference suggests '[o]ver half (53%) of all the top-tier AI researchers are immigrants or foreign nationals currently working in a different country from where they received their undergraduate degrees' (MarcoPolo 2022b). Moreover, while:

> China is the largest source of top-tier researchers, with 29% of these researchers having received undergraduate degrees in China … the majority of those Chinese researchers (56%) go on to study, work, and live in the United States. (ibid)

The study from MarcoPolo, a think tank at the Paulson Institute in Chicago, also includes an analysis of transitions from undergraduate study to postgraduate employment. This suggests that 58.29% of 'top-tier' AI researchers who obtained their undergraduate degree in China went on to graduate study in the US (ibid), while 32.62% stayed for postgraduate employment. Only 3.74% of Chinese undergraduates returned to China for postgraduate work after graduate school in the US (ibid). This suggests a substantial migration of AI 'talent' from China to the US, and, arguably, questionable success for initiatives, such as 'Thousand Talents', that have attempted to entice Chinese nationals back home. However, the analysis also suggests that 31.55% of 'top-tier' AI researchers with Chinese undergraduate degrees continued graduate study in China, while 16.58% went on to postgraduate employment in the country, with only 2.14% going to work in the US. While these numbers are significantly less than the US trajectory, they appear to demonstrate a clear 'internal' route, through which China is producing AI expertise at the very highest level.

However, aside from national comparisons, which most of the 'AI talent tracking' research appears to be focused on, such analyses also convey, not only a sense of the profound connection between China and the US, but also the substantial role that Chinese nationals are playing in the development of AI internationally. A recent *New York Times* article even describes Chinese 'talent' in AI as the US's 'secret weapon' (2021), due to their tendency to emigrate across the Pacific for study and work. As Lee suggests: 'American universities and technology companies have for decades reaped the rewards of the country's ability to attract and absorb talent from around the globe' (Lee Kei Fu 2018, p11), and, as the statistics appear to demonstrate, this talent is arriving predominantly from China. A number of think tanks in the US have begun emphasising this influx of expertise as a key resource to retain, under the assumption that the country may not remain as attractive without continued policy interventions. A report from the CSET suggests:

> More than half of the AI workforce in the United States was born abroad, as were around two-thirds of current graduate students in AI-related fields. Tens of thousands of international students get AI-related degrees at US universities every year. Retaining them, and ensuring a steady future talent inflow, is among the most important things the United States can do to address persistent domestic AI work-force shortages and to remain the global leader in AI.
>
> (Zwetsloot et al. 2019, piii)

Moreover, this report makes it clear that this strategy is directed principally towards China, describing it as an 'AI competitor' (Zwetsloot et al. 2019, piii). Zwetsloot and Peterson further describe this scenario as China's 'immigration disadvantage' (2019).

> [D]espite China's two decades of talent recruitment drives, nationals either do not return or do so part-time, mostly due to workplace politics. Meanwhile, 91 percent of top Chinese students with US AI doctorates are still in the United States five years after graduating.
>
> (Peterson et al. 2021, p37)

Such 'AI talent tracking' appears, therefore, to imagine a domain of high-stakes competition, in which future graduates and professionals skilled in the techniques of AI will be desperate to select the best country in which to supply their coveted expertise. The task of national education policy in this vision appears to be to foster the most accommodating environments, in order that the valuable human capital of 'AI talent' can be put to use in the national interest. As such, the high-profile statistical measure of 'national AI capacity' appears to reinforce a wider imaginary of AI-induced national competition and geopolitical rivalry.

Concluding remarks

This chapter examined the notion of 'AI talent', which serves as an important dimension within the wider sociotechnical imaginaries of AI in China and elsewhere, envisioning an educational 'pipeline' to progress students towards research and work in a future data-driven economy. China appears to have been constructing this vision through a range of educational reforms, including the establishment of 'double first class' universities that can focus on elite AI research and teaching. As such, and following from the previous chapter, Chinese universities are being envisioned as global power houses for AI, modelled nevertheless on successful institutions in the US. As the recent *Education Informatization 2.0 Action Plan* makes clear: '[c]olleges and universities are at the juncture of the first productivity of science and technology, the first resource of talents, and the first driving force of innovation' (MEPRC 2018b).

While the 'Thousand Talents' programme, and many others like it, tends to establish a competitive international environment for scientific expertise, looking further back in history reveals different kinds of relations between the US and China. In pursuit of technical knowledge, many Chinese scholars during the reform period of the early 20th century sought out US universities as sources of insight that could modernise China, and travelled for study with a deep sense of national duty. As such, the relentless comparisons examined across this chapter seem to overlook a hidden history of deep ties between China and the US, and the unparalleled contribution that Chinese nationals have made to the development of AI internationally, and across the Pacific specifically. Rather, this chapter has examined the ways in which the international trajectories of AI expertise appear to have become a source of great concern, and elements within both China and the US seem engrossed in strategies that might entice the world's computer science graduates to bolster their own national agendas. Given the substantial numbers of experts who choose to relocate to the US, the efforts to develop domestic AI education might be seen as part of a wider policy strategy by the Chinese government for 'self-reliance' in various areas of science, technology, and manufacturing (S. Ho 2020). Further, the 14th Five Year Plan (see Xinhua News Agency 2021), published in March 2021, has been interpreted as establishing a substantial shift in science and technology development, towards further self-reliance in technologies such as AI, and a focus on domestic applications (see Grünberg and Brussee 2021).

This chapter further examined the burgeoning area of 'national AI capacity' research, which is establishing a series of statistical measures to classify, compare, and rank countries according to their assumed capabilities to utilise AI. This is another important dimension of the sociotechnical imaginary of AI, and one that appears to reinforce nationalistic visions of the future, in which data-driven technologies straightforwardly enhance a country's ability to compete on the world stage. China, as examined previously, often appears to be a focus of such reports, aimed at deriving an objective, precise, and impartial analysis of the wider visions of cold war rivalry over AI. Furthermore, the standardisation of 'AI capacity' developed through research becomes performative, by establishing the specifications and measures through which future policy-making will undoubtedly seek to raise the profile of particular nation states.

References

Berger, E. (2021). *CSRankings: Computer science rankings.* Available: https://csrankings.org/#/index?ai&vision&mlmining&nlp&ir&world

Cao, C., (2008). China's brain drain at the high end: Why government policies have failed to attract first-rate academics to return. *Asian Population Studies*, 4(3), pp.331–345.

DESE [Department of Education, Skills and Employment]. (2017). Double first-class university and discipline list policy update. Government of Australia. 14 December. https://internationaleducation.gov.au/international-network/china/PolicyUpdates-China/Pages/Double-First-Class-university-and-discipline-listpolicy-update.aspx

Ding, J. (2018). Deciphering China's AI Dream: The context, components, capabilities, and consequences of China's strategy to lead the world in AI. Future of Humanity Institute Report. https://www.fhi.ox.ac.uk/wp-content/uploads/Deciphering_Chinas_AI-Dream.pdf

Goode, K., & Peterson, D. (2022). The US can compete with China in AI education — here's how. *The Hill.* 2 April. https://thehill.com/opinion/education/592658-the-us-can-compete-with-china-in-ai-education-heres-how/

Grünberg, N., & Brussee, V. (2021). China's 14th Five-year plan – strengthening the domestic base to become a superpower. *MERICS Report.* 9 April. Available: https://merics.org/en/short-analysis/chinas-14th-five-year-plan-strengthening-domestic-base-become-superpower

Ho, S. (2020). China's AI efforts suggest tactics in new 'self-reliance' push. *New America.* https://www.newamerica.org/cybersecurity-initiative/digichina/blog/chinas-ai-efforts-suggest-tactics-in-new-self-reliance-push/

IBM. (2022). *IBM global AI adoption index 2022.* https://www.ibm.com/downloads/cas/GVAGA3JP

Jia, H. (2018). What is China's thousand talents plan? *Nature Career Guide China.* https://media.nature.com/original/magazine-assets/d41586-018-00538-z/d41586-018-00538-z.pdf

Koty, A.C. (2022). Vocational education in China: New law promotes sector's growth. *China Briefing.* 19 May. Available: https://www.china-briefing.com/news/vocational-education-in-china-new-law-promotes-sectors-growth/

Lee, K-F. (2018). *AI superpowers: China, silicon valley, and the new world order.* New York: Houghton Mifflin Harcourt.

Liu, Y.-L. (2019). China's AI dreams aren't for everyone. *Foreign Policy.* 13 August. https://foreignpolicy.com/2019/08/13/china-artificial-intelligence-dreams-arent-for-everyone-data-privacy-economic-inequality/

Liu, C. (2021). *China's Artificial intelligence research in figures. Sixth Tone. 7 July. https://www.sixthtone.com/news/1007930*

MarcoPolo. (2022a). https://macropolo.org/digital-projects/chinai/the-talent/

MarcoPolo. (2022b). https://macropolo.org/digital-projects/the-global-ai-talent-tracker/

MEPRC [Ministry of Education of the People's Republic of China]. (2018a). Action Plan for Artificial Intelligence Innovation in Colleges and Universities. Accessed 20 April 2019. http://www.moe.gov.cn/srcsite/A16/s7062/201804/t20180410_332722.html

MEPRC [Ministry of Education of the People's Republic of China] (2018b). Education informatization 2.0 action plan [in Chinese] http://www.moe.gov.cn/srcsite/A16/s3342/201804/t20180425_334188.html

MEPRC [Ministry of Education of the People's Republic of China] (2022). Vocational education law of the People's Republic of China. 1 May. Available: http://www.moe.gov.cn/jyb_sjzl/sjzl_zcfg/zcfg_jyfl/202204/t20220421_620064.html

Nettel, P.F., Annys, R., Westgarth, T., Iida, K., Mbayo, H., Finotto, A., Rahim, S., Petheram, A., Strome, E., Del Pozo, C.M., Neff, G., Puchiu, R., Mohamed, A., Salem, F., Shekhar, R., Nachiappan, K., & Ladak, Y. (2021). *Government AI readiness index 2021.* Oxford Insights Report. https://static1.squarespace.com/static/58b2e92c1e5b6c828058484e/t/61ead0752e7529590e98d35f/1642778757117/Government_AI_Readiness_21.pdf

Peng, T. (2018). Chinese publisher introduces AI textbooks for preschoolers. *Medium.* 5 December. https://medium.com/syncedreview/chinese-publisher-introduces-ai-textbooks-for-preschoolers-b95e1a89cfa0

Peterson, D., Goode, K., & Gehlhaus, D. (2021). AI Education in China and the United States: A comparative assessment. CSET [Centre for Security and Emerging Technology] Issue Brief, September 2021. Available: https://cset.georgetown.edu/wp-content/uploads/CSET-AI-Education-in-China-and-the-United-States-1.pdf

Schiermeier, Q. (2014). China: At a crossroads. *Nature,* 507, 129–131. https://www.nature.com/articles/nj7490-129a

Sensetime. (2022). AI basic education. Available: https://www.sensetime.com/en/product-education-01?categoryId=1169

Sharma, Y. (2013). 'Thousand Talents' academic return scheme under review *University World News.* 25th May. Available: https://www.universityworldnews.com/post.php?story=20130524153852829

Sohu. (2020). Welfare for high school students! Tsinghua Yao class first high school AI textbook, edited by Academician Yao Qizhi, published in autumn. *Sohu.com.* 7 January. https://www.sohu.com/a/365398967_821349

State Council. (2015). Overall plan for promoting the construction of world first class universities and first class disciplines. 24 October. Available: http://www.gov.cn/zhengce/content/2015-11/05/content_10269.htm

Tortois (2022). Global AI Index. Available: https://www.tortoisemedia.com/intelligence/global-ai/

The New York Times. (2021). A U.S. secret weapon in A.I.: Chinese talent. *The New York Times.* 13 April. https://www.nytimes.com/2020/06/09/technology/china-ai-research-education.html

Wang, Y. (2022). AI ranks first in 2022 college entrance examination hotly searched majors! *AI Technology Review.* https://mp.weixin.qq.com/s/xg9VmnGFimFgAz96-l0j_w?fbclid=IwAR2F9tlSFdfjpsIXgsD0MafyN7_BWQnVPd2g8AG7LyDaOjgMC0plf2J_Ues

Wang, Z. (2002). Saving China through science: The science society of China, scientific nationalism, and civil society in Republican China, *Osiris*, 2(17), Science and Civil Society 291–322.

Wray, C. (2020). The threat posed by the Chinese Government and the Chinese Communist Party to the Economic and National Security of the United States. *Federal Bureau of Investigation and the Hudson Institute.* 7 July. https://www.fbi.gov/news/speeches/the-threat-posed-by-the-chinese-government-and-the-chinese-communist-party-to-the-economic-and-national-security-of-the-united-states

Xinhua News Agency (新华社). (2021). The 14th Five-Year Plan for National Economic and Social Development of the People's Republic of China and Outline of the Vision for 2035. 12 March. Available: http://www.gov.cn/xinwen/2021-03/13/content_5592681.htm

Ye, W. (2001). *Seeking modernity in China's name: Chinese students in the United States, 1900–1927.* Redwood City: Stanford University Press.

Zhang, D. Maslej, N., Brynjolfsson, E., Etchemendy, J., Lyons, T., Manyika, J., Ngo, H., Niebles, J.C., Sellitto, M., Sakhaee, E., Shoham, Y. Clark, J., & Perrault, R. (2022), "The AI index 2022 annual report," AI index steering Committee, Stanford Institute for Human-Centered AI, Stanford University. https://aiindex.stanford.edu/wp-content/uploads/2022/03/2022-AI-Index-Report_Master.pdf

Zou, S. (2021). AI now most favored major at universities. *China Daily.* 3 March https://www.chinadaily.com.cn/a/202103/03/WS603ec6baa31024ad0baac412.html

Zweig, D., & Chen, C. (1995). *China's brain drain to the United States: Views of Overseas Chinese students and scholars in the 1990s.* Institute of East Asian Studies: University of California, CA.

Zwetsloot, R., & Peterson, D. (2019). The US-China tech wars: China's immigration disadvantage. *The Diplomat.* 31 December. https://thediplomat.com/2019/12/the-us-china-tech-wars-chinas-immigration-disadvantage/

Zwetsloot, R., Dunham, J., Arnold, Z., & Huang, T. (2019). Keeping top AI talent in the United States. CSET [Centre for Security and Emerging Technology] Report, December 2019. https://cset.georgetown.edu/wp-content/uploads/Keeping-Top-AI-Talent-in-the-United-States.pdf

7 Personalisation, subjectivity, and the Chinese 'self'

Following the previous examination of the broad international flows of talented artificial intelligence (AI) experts, this chapter shifts focus to the individual, and the specific ways students, both in the formal and in the informal sense, are imagined to develop and grow through educational practices involving data-driven technologies. The attention here is on examining imaginaries of the learning subject in China, as produced through the increasing use of AI in education. This examination centres on a contrast between, on the one hand, the idea of 'personalisation', which envisions a particular way of tailoring AI-driven educational content and assessments for individual students, and, on the other, the notion of 'person-making' (Zhao and Deng 2016) in Chinese education, which considers the historical and contemporary ways in which Chinese education has produced particular kinds of learning subjects. This contrast will suggest some significant differences between the notions of 'person-making' and 'personalisation', in the sense of different assumptions about the human condition which underpin these ideas as well as of the very different kinds of teaching and learning practices through which they are presumed to arise. The key purpose of this chapter is therefore to examine the ways in which AI-driven technology is situated within the Chinese educational context, in the sense of being both grounded in traditional education practices and linked to notions of novelty and innovation, and a challenge to the existing order. In these ways, the imaginary of AI-driven education might be viewed, not only in terms of the establishment of particular kinds of educational markets, but also in the sense of playing a substantive role in shaping individuals as particular kinds of learning subjects. Where previous chapters have analysed policies, institutions, and markets related to the future visions of AI and education, this chapter turns attention to the *subjects* of such imaginaries, namely, the students and young people increasingly engaged with data-driven technologies in their everyday educational activity. In this sense, while the previous chapters in this book have attempted to connect policy and the private sector, as well as national development and geopolitical positioning, in the broader sociotechnical imaginaries of AI, this final thematic chapter seeks to draw together some of the ways this wider

DOI: 10.4324/9781003375135-7

future-making functions to shape society and the 'self' through the use of AI in education.

Given that AI which is designed and deployed specifically for educational purposes is, at least on the surface, concerned primarily with the development of individuals (in other words, their 'learning', or perhaps their 'performance' in educational activity), it seems pertinent to begin with questions about what kind of individuals are assumed in the Chinese education system – in other words, questions about the human condition specific to China. Outside of the specific context of China, Pedersen points out the somewhat paradoxical state of affairs in which education is something reserved for the human species exclusively, yet the condition of being human is also assumed to be the 'end product of education' (Pedersen 2010, p241). In other words, only humans enter into education, but we also *become* human through the process. Key questions for the subsequent discussion are therefore what kind of individuals are assumed to enter into education in China and what kind of individuals are such processes presumed to produce? It is important to emphasise that assumptions about the character of the human condition and its relationship to the project of education shift over time, and the discourses which promote, justify, and sometimes decry the use of AI in education are merely the latest in a long line of ideas about the ways educational practices and experiences might be deployed to realise particular kinds of human subjects. Indeed, as we shall see, AI is often promoted in ways that tend to align with outmoded views of education, rather than necessarily offering something novel or innovative to educational practice. In order to examine the extent to which AI technology development aligns with educational theory and practice, this chapter will also examine questions about the purpose of education, drawing principally on the work of Biesta (2009, 2013, 2015). Biesta suggests that 'when we are engaged in decision making about the direction of education we are always and necessarily engaged in value judgements – judgements about what is educationally desirable' (Biesta 2009, p35). Biesta further distinguishes between three domains of educational purpose: *qualification*, referring to the domain of skills acquisition; *socialisation*, signifying the ways individuals become part of society through educational processes; and *subjectification*, which concerns the ways in which individuals become independent and self-directed (2013, 2015). Zhao (2016) uses this framework specifically to develop a notion of education as 'person-making' in the Chinese context, for which both Western and traditional Chinese educational ideas are brought into alignment. However, for Zhao (2016), it is the domain of *subjectification* in particular that is most important, justified on the basis that it is the individual that ends up providing a foundation for, and hence defining, the other domains of *qualification* and *socialisation*. Zhao suggests: 'the kind of human beings coming out of education eventually defines the kind of society, state or economy there can be' (Zhao 2016a, p14). This is the precisely the rationale underpinning this chapter, which is focused on the kind of 'persons' that an AI-infused education is being imagined to produce in China. While there is good reason to focus on the policies and markets of AI, as have a number of the other chapters in this book, it is also worth dwelling on questions about the character of the human condition shaped by the Chinese education system and its increasing use of technology, given that the forming of such persons may ultimately have a foundational impact on the politics and economy of the country in future years.

'Personalisation'

The idea of 'personalisation' features prominently in the discourse around AI in education, being a key term employed by international organisations such as the OECD (see Nemorin et al. 2022). However, within these visions of 'personalised' AI-driven learning, often multiple, sometimes conflicting definitions appear to emerge. On the one hand, 'personalisation' is frequently used to refer to the technical functioning of the software and its ability to serve students with resources and assessments that match their learning needs at a given time – the precise operation of such AI-driven systems will be examined in further detail below. Here, personalisation appears to refer to the idea that AI can deliver an individualised, rather than standardised, learning experience, and in a basic sense draws from the wider trend for recommender systems found in social media. In an educational context, however, AI thus appears to be envisioned, not only to stand in for the figure of the teacher, but also to enhance the teaching role by providing bespoke instruction to individual students, rather than uniform lessons to an entire class. Central to the imaginary of AI in education is therefore a revisioning of the teacher, a point made clear in a recent interview with Richard Tong, Chief Architect at Squirrel AI:

> We want to use AI to teach. The model is not about the teacher any-more. The model has shifted the center of the learning universe to students. It's all about one-on-one instruction, feedback, practice and personalization.
>
> (Tong in Goel and Camacho 2020)

In this view, human teachers are positioned as scarce and inefficient; as Tong further suggests, '[i]n the past, the barrier is that the teacher is a limited resource. It's a resource that we cannot afford to give to every kid, especially those from poorer background' (Tong in Goel and Camacho 2020). AI sup-posedly solves these flaws through its ability, not only to teach potentially infinite numbers of students at the same time, but also to tailor its teaching to individual requirements. This is often referred to as the benefit of 'scale'.

This valuing of the one-to-one pedagogical relationship is established in promotional research elsewhere, such as Luckin et al.'s report on AI for education in collaboration with Pearson, which extols the virtues of 'an intelligent, personal tutor for every learner' (2016, p24). Sir Anthony Seldon, an influential educator in the UK, has also promoted 'the possibility of an Eton or Wellington[1] education for all' in which 'everyone can have the very best teacher' provided be 'adaptive machines that adapt to individuals' (Seldon cited in von Radowitz 2017). As such, 'personalising' AI is frequently imagined in terms of its capacity to surpass the limitations of human teachers, and offer an enhanced and elite version of the experience of being taught. Founder of Squirrel AI (examined in Chapters 3 and 4), Li Haoyang, describes aims to 'provide each child with a super-power AI teacher that is the combination of Einstein and Socrates, that way it feels like she has more than 100 teachers in front of her' (Li quoted in van Hooijdonk 2019). This primary vision of educational AI, offering almost super-human expertise that far transcends the abilities of the average teacher, aligns with promotional discourse elsewhere about the promise of data-driven teaching. The international publishing company Pearson has also replicated this vision, with their director of artificial intelligence, Milena Marinova, suggesting: 'every student would have that Aristotle tutor, that one-on-one, and every teacher would know everything there is to know about every subject' (Marinova cited in Olson 2018). In these visions, not only is 'personalisation' cast as the ability to supply an abundance of AI-driven super-human teachers, but the agency of individual human teachers and educational institutions seems to be pushed into the background. There is little here to discern the ways in which professional teachers and schools might have influence over the design of such personalising AI systems. What is particularly interesting about this educational imaginary is that it is established through an assumption of granting more agency to the student, with the idea that they are 'centralised' in the educational process. However, as the next section will explore in detail, personalising AI appears to function in ways that suggest the very opposite.

Friesen (2020) provides an important critique of personalisation. Questioning the idea that a one-to-one relationship between teacher and student is indisputably the most beneficial form of education, Friesen (2020) highlights a 'mythology' of personal teaching throughout European history (from Socrates, to Comenius, and finally to Rousseau) that has continued into the contemporary imaginaries of computer assisted learning. Rather than simply innovation, Friesen argues, one-to-one teaching is 'a kind of repetitive continuity that educational innovators generally see themselves as leaving behind' (2020, p4).

Importantly for now, amongst the claims of AI's superiority over human teaching, alternative views of personalisation often surface. A notable example is the imaginary that AI will provide teachers with more time in the classroom to focus on individual teaching, by taking on routine tasks. Hao, in an article about Squirrel AI, sums up this position succinctly:

> the 21st-century classroom should bring out the strengths and interests of each person, rather than impart a canonical set of knowledge more

suited for the industrial age... AI, in theory, could make this easier. It could take over certain rote tasks in the classroom, freeing teachers up to pay more attention to each student.

(Hao 2019)

Significant here is that, rather than the AI itself providing innovative or enhanced learning, this vision of 'personalisation' reverts back to teachers as the ultimate source of authentic teaching, while the technology is positioned subserviently, as a low-level assistant. This imaginary doesn't appear to straightforwardly align with the above vision of sophisticated, superhuman AI, able to solve the problem of teachers being limited resources. Rather, this alternative vision of personalisation seems to rely on highly skilled human teachers as the principal means of providing individualised learning. This directly contrasts with the vision of AI as supplying expert pedagogy, in ways that reduce the need for skilled teachers, exemplified in Tong's analogy of GPS technology for driving:

With GPS, you don't need to be a super-knowledgeable human driver anymore. Instead, you can have a decent driver that does not have a lot the mapping information, as long as the GPS is available.

(Tong in Goel and Camacho 2020)

Li confirms this vision through a similar analogy suggesting that future teachers will be like airline pilots: '[t]hey will monitor the readouts while the algorithm flies the plane, and for the most part they will play a passive role' (Li cited in Hao 2019). In this interview, Li goes on to suggest that AI would allow human teachers to focus on communication and emotional learning. In these overlapping visions of personalised AI, therefore, the teacher appears both central and peripheral, valued and downgraded, a knowledgeable expert and a passive facilitator. Furthermore, personalisation itself seems to carry multiple meanings, being a way of centralising students in the educational process, a sense of empowerment through direct access to a more-than-human form of expertise, as well as a route to more interactions with a human teacher.

Another significant vision of personalised learning makes association with the wider notion of 'disruptive' technologies. Interviewed in a report by Nesta, Tong, compares:

Squirrel's transformation of the public education system to the way ride-sharing companies such as Uber and Didi changed public transportation systems – providing the same service through a more convenient and personalised pathway.

(Tong cited in Liu 2020)

Here the vision of personalisation appears to be related to technological transformations of the economy, in which individuals are supplied with tailored services. This draws on a core set of assumptions about the ways in which data-driven platforms have been able to make a whole range of sectors more efficient, improve individual consumer experience, and enhance society more generally, assumptions that are being increasingly contested through research on, for example, labour practices and regulation (Wells 2020). Here AI-driven personalisation is recast again as a form of consumerism, in which educational companies are disrupting the inefficiencies of traditional education, and authentic learning is remodelled as a practice of convenience and efficiency.

In order to further understand how these imaginaries of 'personalised' learning are materialising in education, and the ways they are shaping student subjectivity, it is important to examine the specific functioning of AI-driven educational platforms.

'Knowledge spaces' and pedagogical control

Squirrel AI, as one of most prominent educational AI companies in China (discussed in detail in Chapters 3 and 4), provides a key example of personalising or adaptive software.[2] Other notable examples of personalising software include the ALEKS[3] (Assessment and Learning in Knowledge Spaces) platform, designed at the University of California, Irvine, and subsequently bought by educational publishing company McGraw Gill Education, and Century Tech,[4] a UK-based company that claims a grounding in AI and neuroscience research. All of these AI-driven platforms operate in a similar way, involving the use of machine learning techniques to recommend specific resources or assessment activities to users, derived from analyses of individual and group behaviours within the software. Following from the above visions of one-to-one AI-driven tuition, such automated recommendation is designed specifically to replace the need for human teachers to serve up resources and assessments. Key to this functioning is the 'knowledge domain' or 'knowledge space', which establishes a mathematical representation of all knowledge within a defined topic area. This mathematical representation is produced by dividing up a given topic into basic elements – Century, for example, terms the individual elements 'nuggets' – so that optimal combinations and sequences of learning material can be derived. For example, AI software offering a course on algebra has a predefined 'knowledge space' comprising all aspects of the topic, broken down into individual elements, such as the rules, symbols, and concepts associated with this branch of mathematics. Students undergo an initial assessment designed to determine their current level of knowledge with respect to the established 'knowledge space', for example, analysing whether they already understand basic equations or the concept of variables. Combining this assessment data with the mathematical representation of the topic allows the AI software to position a particular student within the 'knowledge space', calculating not only which areas are already understood and which areas need to be learned, but also the optimal path through the new material, so that the entire subject matter can be completed in the most efficient manner. Squirrel AI's system is described thusly:

> Each course is subdivided into the smallest possible conceptual pieces, such that the algorithm can diagnose student gaps in understanding as precisely as possible, adjusting learning pathways in real time. Middle school maths, for example, is broken into 10,000 'knowledge points' such as rational numbers, the properties of a triangle and the Pythagorean theorem.
>
> (Liu 2020)

As Joleen Liang of Squirrel AI emphasises, the AI system focuses exclusively on identified weakness following the initial assessment (Bloomberg 2019). The calculation of this optimal path is what is termed 'personalisation', or 'adaptation', as learning resources and assessments are served up to the student, depending on their position within the 'knowledge space', and the calculated route forward, which also incorporates data from previous students' trajectories through the software. Siemens explains how the 'knowledge domain' underpins the ability to track and guide learners within AI software:

> Once knowledge domains have been articulated or mapped, learner data, profile information, and curricular data can be brought together and analyzed to determine learner knowledge in relation to the knowledge structure of a discipline. Data trails and profiles, in relation to curriculum in a course, can be analyzed and used as a basis for prediction, intervention, personalization, and adaptation.
>
> (Siemens 2013, p1389)

The learning development of a particular student, and their specific trajectory through the AI software, is therefore a matter of prediction, intervention, personalisation, and adaptation, as opposed to personal choice and agency.

An additionally important point here is that the mathematical construction of the 'knowledge space' presumes an intrinsic value to the modularisation of knowledge, and the idea that a given topic can be subdivided and reassembled with almost infinite variety. While in one sense this is justified on the grounds of offering students an optimal and individualised pathway through a given topic of study, and presumably a better chance of completing the learning material, such modularisation is determined by the AI, and therefore constitutes an additional act of control over knowledge. It is also important to emphasise here that the 'knowledge space' is not an aspect of the software made available or visible to the student. Rather, it is part of the underlying functioning, beneath the user interface. This means that students typically encounter only the specific materials or assessments served up by the AI software, usually accompanied by some form of analytics that visualise completed modules or lessons. Such an arrangement might be interpreted as an additional level of control, where students are denied access to the central means of determining their position within a given topic of study, as well as their future trajectory through it. Indeed, access to such a map or diagram seems unnecessary where 'optimal' decisions about learning pathways are made by the AI.

In these ways, the 'knowledge spaces' that underpin personalising AI platforms in education appear to be strict sites of control, raising significant questions about the extent to which students have agency in such educational arrangements. In order to examine agency further, particularly with a concern for the kind of student subjectivity that might emerge from such spaces of control, the next section turns to a concept of education purpose.

Student agency and subjectification

One key conceptualisation of educational purpose is that developed by Biesta (2009, 2013, 2015), who suggests three dimensions: *qualification*, which relates to the domain of skills acquisition; *socialisation*, which concerns the ways individuals become part of society; and, finally, *subjectification*, focused on the kind of individuality and personhood fostered through a particular education structure. For Biesta (2009, 2013, 2015), all education necessarily involves all three purposes, but specific instances are likely to emphasise some over others, or render each purpose in a slightly different way. For example, forms of education that are critical of testing, measurement, and outcomes tend to emphasise the socialisation and/or the subjectification dimensions by foregrounding social interaction or individual development, while downplaying that of qualification by rejecting traditional forms of educational assessment. Another key aspect of Biesta's theory, and a vital part of understanding the three domains of educational purpose, is the distinction made between education and learning. Questioning the reorientation of educational institutions around the assumption of a self-directing 'learner', Biesta suggests 'learning' itself to be 'basically a process term' that refers to 'processes and activities but is open – if not empty – with regard to content and direction' (Biesta 2009, p39). In other words, a discourse of 'learnification' (Biesta 2009; 2013) has expunged any sense of educational purpose from the act of learning, and in its place assumed the figure of a self-serving individual, reflective of a wider neoliberal framing of society. In contrast, Biesta suggests that education 'always raises the question of its purpose' (Biesta 2015, p84). And, furthermore, 'when we are engaged in decision making about the direction of education we are always and necessarily engaged in value judgements – judgements about what is educationally desirable' (Biesta 2009, p35). In other words, while learnification privileges individual student desire, education necessitates collective reasoning over values and purposes, and seeks to (re)orient the practice around teaching and the teacher. As such, to exclusively portray education in terms of learning limits the extent to which all of Biesta's domains of purpose can be fulfilled, and tends to privilege *qualification*. Only with education, so Biesta (ibid.) argues, can collective ideals be derived about how individuals become part of society, or how they develop and mature as subjects. Biesta further defines socialisation as 'the many ways in which, through education, we become members of and part of particular social, cultural and political "orders"' (2009, p40), and subjectification as concerning 'the kind of subjectivity – or kinds of subjectivities – that are made possible as a result of particular educational arrangements and configurations' (Biesta 2009, 41). Biesta further describes subjectification as having:

> an orientation towards emancipation – that is, towards ways of doing and being that do not simply accept the given order, but have an orientation towards the change of the existing order so that different ways of doing and being become possible.
>
> (Biesta 2013, p6)

Education, therefore, as distinct from the individualistic and self-directed activities of learning, is central to the ways Biesta envisions the full scope and richness of educational purpose.

These three dimensions of purpose provide a useful framework through which to assess the extent to which agency and subjectivity are fostered through the use of AI-driven platforms, and specifically the structuring function of the 'knowledge space'. First, given that 'knowledge spaces' predefine the limit and boundary of knowledge within a particular topic of study, as detailed in the previous section, such 'personalisation' would appear to have significant limitations concerning the ability of students to engage in educational purposes beyond mere qualification – in particular, where all legitimate and authoritative knowledge is already 'known' by the software, and the student's task is simply to engage with the material served up by the 'personalising' algorithm. The extent to which the learning subject can develop is therefore already determined by the 'knowledge space' within the AI software, leaving no ostensible room to grow and mature in ways not already predefined. This appears to stand in direct contrast to Biesta's notions of emancipation, and the ability to learn and develop in ways that transcend the educational relationship. Such an expansive and liberatory sense of personal development does not seem possible where the domain of knowledge has already been calculated and defined. Furthermore, Biesta (2013) appears to imply that students, if they are to develop authentically as subjects, must contribute to, participate in, and ultimately shape knowledge, as opposed to simply acquiring it within a controlled and predetermined space.

Relatedly then, the capacity for agency afforded to the student in such systems has substantial connotations for the sense of subjectivity that might emerge from an AI-infused education. The ability to make choices about what to learn appears to be significantly curtailed through the establishment of the 'knowledge space' and the automated calculation of 'personalised' pathways. As examined above, rather than the student choosing where to begin the study of a given topic, the AI software determines the starting position through the initial assessment. Subsequently, movement through the learning materials and assessments is also strictly controlled, determined by the calculation of a 'personalised' pathway. In this way, such AI systems might be aligned with what Biesta describes as a *monological* form of pedagogy, a learning scenario in which:

> the teacher knows and students do not know yet; where it is the task of the teacher to explain the world to the students and where it is the task of the students to ultimately become as knowledgeable as the teacher. In this set-up, there is a clear learning task for the student – a task which is basically reproductive in that it is aimed at the acquisition of the insights of the teacher emancipator.
>
> (Biesta 2013, p10)

Such a focus on learning as reproduction, rather than a deeper engagement with the idea of the developing subject, 'tends to domesticate rather than to emancipate' (Biesta 2013, p9), where emancipation is associated with a more profound sense of the development of subjectivity. The monological form of pedagogy is contrasted with a *dialogical* form, for which Biesta (2013) draws on the work of Paulo Freire to suggest 'a process of the collective discovery of oppressive structures, processes and practices' (Biesta 2013, p10). Indeed, in Freire's vision of dialogic pedagogy, teachers and students are positioned as 'co-subjects' (1972, p135). Opportunities for dialogue and the co-production of knowledge do not thus appear to be available in the functioning of the 'knowledge space'. In contrast, a monological form of teaching appears to be rearticulated in the form of persistent tracking and 'diagnosis', as suggested in the following description of Squirrel AI:

> We continually diagnose students as they're learning. We track keystrokes so that we know where you are, how far, how fast you're solving a problem, and other relevant knowledge. Then we calculate the probability that you're going to be able to solve the next question, and use that to diagnose the student learner profile, so that we build this continuous learning profile.
>
> (Tong in Goel and Camacho 2020)

Here, student behaviour within the software platform is constantly monitored, seemingly with the aim of coaching students to be able to reproduce the knowledge points already defined within the AI system. Learning becomes the exclusive practice of replicating the machine, with little opportunity to think differently, or to use the acquired knowledge to transcend the rigid framework of the 'knowledge space'. In this way, personalising AI platforms seem to be severely limiting to the broad ideals of education, and a concern for the development of fully formed human subjects. Such limitations are, of course, not exclusive to China, with the previously mentioned ALEKS and Century platforms deploying very similar forms of personalisation elsewhere. However, as outlined above, powerful visions of personalising AI seem to be particularly prominent in China, promising one-to-one relationships with super-human teachers, and straightforward solutions to educational inequalities. As has also been discussed across this book, education appears to be embroiled in a wider government-endorsed sociotechnical imaginary of AI, in which the technology delivers instrumental enhancements, not only to a future data-driven economy, but also to the educational 'pipeline' that feeds it. It is such a powerful vision of the future that appears to be materialising in the 'knowledge space', and authorising the increasing use of personalising platforms.

Nevertheless, it remains important to connect these future visions of 'personalising' AI with the 'persons' assumed to be involved. For this purpose, the final sections of the chapter will briefly outline a history of the 'self' in China.

The divided self

As suggested previously in this book, for a country with such a rich history as China, the question of where one might begin a historical perspective often presents a significant quandary. However, in the case of a discussion of education and its relation to the human condition, Confucius is probably the most obvious, and most important place to begin. As Zhao suggests, 'almost from the beginning of Chinese civilization, Confucius was accepted as the single most important source of Chinese political ideological and educational ideas' (2016, p15 citing Lee 2000). It is beyond the scope of this book to provide a comprehensive analysis of Confucian ideas and their impact on education; however, a general summary is key to establishing an approximate sense of the individual in Chinese culture, broadly conceived, across what is in reality a vast area of established scholarship (Lee 2000; Goldin 2014). Nevertheless, one might contend that central to Confucianism are the ideals of personal morality, social order, and principled governance, and the sense in which these values are deeply interconnected. This interconnectedness, or one might say harmony, is demonstrated by what is perhaps the most well-known idea attributed to Confucius, that of emphasising the ordered relationships of the family as a model for ideal government. In other words, the ideal individual is one who is fundamentally aware of their particular position within the structured family unit, striving to fulfil it as best they can, while that very arrangement of cohesive (and hierarchical) relationships maintains the wider social order, and (particularly for the vital relationship of father and son) is the explicit model for state governance, and the connection between Emperor and subject. Importantly, what this arrangement does is link the everyday conduct of individuals to the wider sense of a unified, functioning, and harmonious society. Zhao further notes the eight-stage process of traditional Confucian education:

> gewu 格物 (investigating things), zhizhi 致知 (extending knowledge), yichen 意诚 (straightening the will), xinzheng 心正 (rectifying the mind), xiushen 修身 (cultivating the self), qijia 齐家 (regulating the family), zhiguo 治国 (governing the state), qitianxia 平天下 (harmonizing the world).
>
> (Zhao 2016a, p15)

As such, one might suggest that the Confucian model of the individual is thoroughly 'another-oriented' (Zhao 2016a, p15), as opposed to a more Western notion of individualism as self-realisation. Adopted as the underlying set of principles for the education system in ancient China, Confucianism thus guided students directly towards integration in Chinese culture, bound the different dimensions of society together, and ultimately served to 'maintain Chinese civilisation' (Zhao 2016a, p15). The practical realisation of this societal upkeep was the civil service examination system, which, at least on the surface, provided the basis for meritocratic governance, where talented individuals could fulfil the ultimate purpose of their Confucian education by contributing to the running of the state.

As also outlined in previous chapters, it is the often turbulent events of the 20th century in China that offer more direct insight into the contemporary Chinese subject. The three key periods of China's modern history that have been explored across this book are additionally relevant here: the reformism that ushered in the Republic of China until 1949; the establishment of the PRC and Maoist socialism; and perhaps most importantly the market reforms beginning in the late 1970s. Lin (2013) identifies the first of these periods as crucial in forming the modern Chinese identity:

> It was the rise of revolutionary nationalism after the first Opium War of 1840 which forced China to be integrated into the world market, indeed along with it internationalism of alliance with oppressed peoples within and without China proper, that conferred on the modern Chinese identity a cohesive self-consciousness. This new and superseding sense of collective identity came into being in terms of the 'Chinese nation' and the 'Chinese people' through China's twentieth-century revolutions.
>
> (Lin 2013, p5)

The conflict and political reform across this period often involved direct challenges to the established Confucian social order and sense of harmony, and therefore radical reconsiderations of the human condition and sense of 'self' in China. As Kleinman et al. (2011) suggest, these new formulations of the individual were also directly linked to the emerging ideas of Chinese nationhood: '[a]t the turn of the twentieth century, Chinese intellectuals and political reformers saw the necessity of liberating the individual from the small and inward family circle in order to serve the nation-state' (Kleinman et al. 2011, p8). As Kleinman at al. (2011) further note, the dramatic shift from a long-established Confucian tradition to the new sense of 20th-century individualism resulted in something of a loss of identity for Chinese people. In particular, it is claimed that the Chinese sense of self thus became divided, between an identity that was focused on individuality and another identity that was concerned with the wider social and political environment. Kleinman et al. suggest of Chinese citizens in this period: 'the individual has a dual-self, the small self centred on personal interest and the great self based on the interest of the nation; the small self should always be secondary and submissive to the great self' (Kleinman et al. 2011, p9). Importantly, as Kleinman et al. (2011) argue, this vision of the divided self was not only maintained throughout the various upheavals of the 20th century in China, but it also remains central to contemporary governance and citizenship. Furthermore, this division suggests a rather fundamental connection between the self and the wider social and political environment that appears to have direct relevance to the policy-driven visions of AI, and in particular the overt framing of AI 'talent' as in service to national strategy. Without relying on the uncritical assumption that individualism is an exclusively European tradition, it is worth acknowledging that within a culture that is at least partially 'another-oriented', envisioning an education that explicitly serves a national interest may not appear particularly radical.

The traumatic experiences[5] of this period also had substantial implications for China's education system, which sought to address the sense of humiliation and defeat with the importation of Western ideas and technology. This 'modernisation' eventually involved the rapid adoption of a Western model for the school system, 'together with Western curricular structure, theory, and practice' (Zhou and Deng 2016, p3), in ways that failed to resolve the underlying tensions between China's traditional Confucian education the new ideas of individuality. Furthermore, Zhao contends that such reformist movements were underpinned by the phrase 中体西用 ('zhongti xiyong') put forward by Qing official Zhang Zhidong, translated as 'using Western technology as a means to strengthen the Confucian Chinese substance' (2016, p17). For Zhao (2016), the significance of this statement was in the way it established a very particular view of Western power as derived from 'practical means and instruments (qiwu 器物)' (2016, p17). As such, the dominant reformers sought to adopt Western science and technology as a supplement to existing Chinese culture, without an authentic understanding of its underlying philosophy. As Zhou suggests, this 'led to the importation of a superficial and distorted form of modern Western civilisation' (2016, p17), which ultimately resulted in a loss of ground for the Chinese sense of self, caught between a long-established Confucian tradition and a hastily adopted view of European science and individualism. There is an important parallel here in the recent ambitions for AI development in China. In the sense that Western technical practices were viewed as straightforward and instrumental ways to achieve national development, Zhao's (2016) account of the early 20th-century reform period in China appears to mirror many of the ways AI has been imagined as a solutionist and determinist technology, able to induce a radical transformation in the Chinese economy. For Zhao (2016), calls for the hasty uptake of Western science and technology resulted in a radicalisation of the intellectual climate of the time, and the culpability for China's woes being increasingly attributed to traditional Confucian values. It is pressing, therefore, to remain attentive to the educational practices and ideas that might be marginalised in the rush for progressive AI.

While the foundational years of the PRC under Maoist socialism arguably left no room for any sense of the individual, at least at the level of state ideology (Kleinman et al. 2011), the new divided self was able to function as a citizen due to the maintenance and prioritisation of a 'great self', concerned with the interests of the nation rather than personal desires. As Law suggests, 'the CPC-led state used education to nurture and equip "new socialist persons" to be collectivistic, rather than individual, selves, living and functioning to serve a new socialist China' (Law 2016, p42). Education was thus positioned as an engine of Lin's (2006) triadic framework, driving the nationalism, socialism, and developmentalism of the state, but also, in the process, shaping the sense of self as collectively minded.

The entrepreneurial self

Perhaps most important for the interest in contemporary education and AI are the political reforms under Deng Xiaoping, and their substantial influence on the unfolding Chinese sense of self. Broadly, the imposition of a market economy, as opposed to centralised state control, engendered fundamental shifts, not only in the ways individuals were perceived to be positioned in relation to the state and each other, but also in the sense of civic responsibility and opportunity for personal interest. As Kleinman et al. contend:

> Chinese society since the 1980s is characterized by high mobility and the reformation of social groups; consequently, the remaking of the moral person has also undergone a dynamic process of restratifying and repositioning the self.
>
> (Kleinman et al. 2011, p11)

More specifically, the reforms of this period meant that citizens were able, not only to work outside of the state controlled economic sector, and thus pursue working lives that could be somewhat disengaged from nationalistic agendas, but also to become consumers within newly formed markets, in which a sense of individuality could be nurtured through different lifestyle choices (Kleinman et al. 2011). Alongside these shifts was also the substantial 'marketisation of education', which formed one of the three major state reforms of the 1990s, alongside the privatisation of housing and similar economic reorganisations in medical care (Kleinman et al. 2011, p15). The education system thus not only aligned with transformations in wider society, but also functioned to drive a logic of individual choice, self-interest, and competition in China. As detailed in Chapter 3, this period is precisely when private education (re)emerged in China, and the fervent marketing of English- tuition can be further understood in terms of the burgeoning sense of Chinese individuality and personal choice, as companies competed for the attention of those seeking to develop their individual skills and capacities. Importantly then, the emerging market in which a company such as New Oriental (discussed in detail in Chapters 3 and 4) would thrive was one only possible where the sense of self could be understood as enterprising, and able to engage in self-development and personal refinement, in this case through the learning of English. While such market reform, or neoliberalism, has received much attention in scholarship concerned with its ideological ramifications, and the extent to which notions of reduced state control rearticulate the liberal humanist subject in terms of increased individuality and personal responsibility (e.g. Rose 1999), the key point here is that these shifts were experienced particularly intensely in China due to its recent history under Maoist socialism, and also, arguably, its deeper and latent traditions of Confucianism. As discussed above, the sense of self that developed across 20th-century China was not only underpinned by the 'another oriented' traditions of Confucianism, but also shaped by the wider political priorities of nationalism and socialism, such that the liberal form of individualism that seemed to emerge in the 1980s and 1990s did so with considerable novelty. Of course, China's continued engagement with market reforms was not simply a matter of internal economic reorganisations and their impact of the sense of self, but also related to increasing internationalisation (Law 2016). This enterprising self provides perhaps the clearest context through which to understand the proliferation of AI in the contemporary private after-school sector in China, and the wider imaginary of 'smart' technologies and personalising platforms that serve the demands of the country's competitive student populations. It is only through a self that is able to conceive of self-improvement that AI-driven personalisation becomes possible, as a vision of future education, and as a software platform efficiently delivering learning materials. That the enterprising self is relatively novel in China may be one contribution to the pace and fervour through which the imaginary of AI-infused education appears to be taking hold.

These broad phases are, of course, not suggested to have simply replaced one another as definitive models of the 'self' in China, but rather to have shaped the sense of individuality over time. As such, Kleinman et al. (2011) frame the Chinese sense of self as a site of conflict, across broadly Confucianist (traditional), nationalist and socialist (modern), as well as individualist (contemporary) ideas, all of which are still at play. While such disparate identities might be construed as conflicting, it is important to perceive the ways in which the combination of modern and contemporary sensibilities have aligned with different dimensions of the sociotechnical imaginary of AI. A divided Chinese identity, arguably, appears well suited to engage in both a government-endorsed vision of AI-driven education for national development and a commercial vision of 'smart' platforms for individual betterment. Furthermore, personalised learning driven by AI is also, as Yan and Yang claim, directly linked to Confucian teaching:

> Personalized learning is the learning mode that conforms to human nature. Confucius, China's most famous teacher and a great educator, was the first to propose 'teaching students according to their aptitudes' so that everyone can receive a matching education according to their abilities and characteristics. Artificial intelligence technology provides advantages for 'teaching students according to their aptitude'.
>
> (Yan and Yang 2021, p422)

In this way, and as also suggested above, the imaginary of AI-driven personalised learning appears rather adaptable, and able to assume modes of education that align with the traditional, modern, and contemporary Chinese self. Nevertheless, the historical perspectives outlined here suggest a much richer sense of Chinese identity and subjectivity than is generally assumed by the promotional discourse around personalising AI-driven platforms. Rather, the vision of personalised learning seems to cast students as uniform users of software platforms, and passive recipients of algorithmically delivered knowledge.

The creative self

While powerful, policy- and market- driven imaginaries of an AI-infused education appear rampant in China, the country is certainly not deprived of alternative visions of education. Indeed, the notion of 'personalisation' (examined previously as a term central to the imaginary of educational AI) can be traced back to education policy reform in China in the 1990s which sought to challenge the focus on exam preparation and rote learning (Liu and He 2012).[6] Liu and He further contend:

> the rigorous examination-oriented education, widely criticised by parents, teachers and students, has been a stumbling block for the

cultivation of creative talents who are the backbone of social development and national prosperity.

(Liu and He 2012, p132)

As Lin (2017) further notes, education policies criticising 'examination-oriented education' (2017, p148) were being published in the early 1990s, culminating in the suzhi jiaoyu (素质教育, translated as 'quality education', 'moral education', or 'well rounded education') policy published in 1999. This attempted to instil broad reforms, variously interpreted as oriented towards '"creativity" (chuangzao xing 创造性), "individuality" (gexing 个性), "self-management" (zizhu 自主), "education democracy" (jiaoyu minzhu 教育民主) and "people-first" (renmen 人本)' (2017, p155–156) forms of education. Such policies have been interpreted as promoting the 'personalisation' of education in China, by encouraging institutions to 'adjust education to meet the needs of every student' and 'acknowledge every student's individual differences and teach them accordingly' (Liu and He 2012, p132). Liu and He emphasise curriculum reform in Shanghai in the late 1990s as a prominent example, which aimed to:

> transform the role of the students from passive receivers of knowledge to active participants in learning, to improve students' capacity for creativity and self-development, and to fully achieve their potential.
>
> (Liu and He 2012, p134)

Notably, this definition of personalisation appears to align with Biesta's notion of subjectivity discussed previously, particularly in the way that active participation, self-development, and liberation are implied. More contemporary educational ideas are abundant. Zhou and Deng (2016) propose a revitalisation of Confucian education and the notion of 'person-making', as a way of countering vocationalisation and exam orientation, and explicitly fostering Biesta's concept of subjectivity. Calls for a 'New Basic Education', based around ideas of constructivism, and driven by 'backbone' teachers, are also prominent (Bu and Han 2019). Furthermore, as Tatlow describes, the phrase 'Double Creativity' (双创 'shuangchuang'), derived from recent government interest in creative forms of education, now 'permeates daily life and is seen on red banners, heard in state media and is an educational goal in schools' (2019, p4). Notably, creativity appears to be coveted specifically for its potential to drive the development of leading technology companies (ibid). As such, according to Tatlow, 'a balancing act is underway between subjective human empowerment and objective political and economic power' (2019, p4). In these ways, debates about the state of education in China continue, often with numerous arguments for a 'well rounded' education that pays less attention to the infamous Gaokao. In other words, there are rich alternatives to the more instrumental visions of AI-driven personalisation, and the tightly controlled domain of the 'knowledge space', as outlined previously. These alternatives may lay the groundwork for alternative futures of educational AI in China, embracing a broader vision of 'personhood' in the sense of a 'deep cultural and civilizational engagement and dialogue' (Zhao 2016b, p167), as the guiding rationale for data-driven intervention in Chinese education, as opposed to the narrow tendencies to 'personalise' learner experiences for the purposes of the efficient memorisation of curricula. The key question for the future will be which version of education gets made.

Concluding remarks

This chapter examined the implications of the relationships between AI and education for the notion of human subjectivity. 'Personalisation' has surfaced as a key term in the promotional narratives of educational AI, revealing conflicting visions of the role of the teacher, and a valorisation of one-to-one pedagogical relationships. The chapter also analysed 'knowledge spaces', being one of the central functions of AI-driven personalisation, in which a given topic is rendered into a mathematical representation of 'knowledge points', and students are directed according to optimal, algorithmically derived pathways. Such an arrangement appears to have substantial implications for student agency and subjectivity, given the ways knowledge is predefined and delimited, and student pathways are rigidly controlled. Drawing on Biesta's concept of education purpose, personalising AI appears oriented only towards qualification, and unable to contend with notions of socialisation and subjectification, thus dramatically limiting the ways the technology can support broader understandings of education.

The final sections of the chapter outline a brief history of the self, suggesting the relevance of a 'divided self' drawing from Confucian and Western traditions, and an 'enterprising self' deriving from the market-reform period. These insights suggest some of the ways in which AI imaginaries might have taken hold in China, specifically by accommodating a distributed and conflicting sense of Chinese self. However, more profoundly, the historical insights outlined in this chapter suggest a much richer sense of identity and subjectivity than appears to be acknowledged by 'personalising' AI software. This excavation of the Chinese 'self' might thus be viewed as a surfacing of histories that have been obscured by the imaginaries of AI. Finally, a 'creative self' was outlined to acknowledge long-standing calls for alternatives to China's focus on testing and rote learning, and suggested as the groundwork from which alternative visions of education might shape the future of AI.

As a final reflection, Zhao and Deng (2016), Zhou (2016), Zhang (2016), and Ke (2016) draw on the rich traditions of Confucian education in conjunction with Biesta's concept of subjectivity, to suggest ways in which Chinese education might be reanimated with a renewed sense of purpose. Specifically, Zhang suggests the concepts of socialisation and subjectification as a way of addressing 'the dichotomy between "the small self" and "the big self" in the different periods of China's modern transformation' (2016, p77). In other words, the tension between the educational purposes of self-development and societal cohesion mirrors the fundamental conflicts underpinning Chinese contemporary identity, chiefly that between an other-oriented Confucian tradition and a Western sense of liberal individualism. As Zhao and Deng (2016), Zhou (2016), Zhang (2016), and Ke (2016) argue, this tension can be resolved, not only through education, but specifically by focusing on subjectification, as the key purpose, and the foundation for achieving both a cohesive society and a productive domain of skills acquisition. Biesta also distinguishes subjectivity, suggesting 'any education worthy of its name should always contribute to processes of subjectification that allow those being educated to become more autonomous and independent in their thinking and acting' (2009, p41). The fostering of a 'well rounded' and creative subject is therefore a central challenge for the future of AI in education, which may need to look beyond the vision of personalisation, and the 'knowledge spaces' of control that seem to thus far dictate the direction of the technology.

Notes

1 Eton and Wellington refer to private schools in the UK, used here to infer an elite education. It is also notable that Seldon served as headmaster of Wellington College.
2 For the purposes of this chapter 'adaptative' learning will be considered operationally synonymous with 'personalisation'. Both terms essentially describe automated systems which attempt to provide individualised resources and assessments to students. One of the key differences is that 'personalisation' has a longer history of usage in educational theory, whereas 'adaptive learning' tends to be applied to uses of technology specifically. Indeed, that 'personalisation' is often used synonymously with 'adaptive learning' appears to demonstrate the ways the former term has been co-opted by promotional AI discourse, in order to align the supposed benefits of the technology to established ideas in education.
3 See https://www.aleks.com/about_aleks
4 See https://www.century.tech/about-us/
5 Zhao (2016) examines the ways in which these events humiliated the literati of the Qing dynasty, who pushed for immediate reform and modernisation of the state, through the Gongche Shangshu movement (公车上书) and subsequent Hundred Days' Reform (戊戌变法). These were precursors, not only to the eventual overthrowing of the Qing monarchy and the establishment of a republic, but also to the establishment of a 'countrywide modern school system' (Zhao 2016a, p18) in 1901, and the abolishment of the civil service examination in 1905.
6 However, Liu and He also make deeper historical connections, suggesting 'the principle of teaching students in accordance with their aptitudes' (2012, p130) as a foundational Confucian method, as well as making links with the reformist period of the early 20th century, where Chinese students studying abroad brought back Western educational theories of self-actualisation, such as those of John Dewey – this student emigration is examined further in Chapter 5.

References

Biesta, G.J.J. (2009). Good education in an age of measurement: On the need to reconnect with the question of purpose in education. *Educational Assessment, Evaluation and Accountability*, 21, 33–46. https://doi.org/10.1007/s11092-008-9064-9

Biesta, G.J.J. (2013). Interrupting the politics of learning. *Power and Education*, 5(1), 4–15. https://doi.org/10.2304/power.2013.5.1.4

Biesta, G.J.J. (2015). What is education for? On good education, teacher judgement, and educational professionalism. *European Journal of Education*, 50(1), 75–87. https://doi.org/10.1111/ejed.12109

Bloomberg. (2019). How squirrel AI learning is shaking up education in China. *Bloomberg* Available: https://youtu.be/eHab0NvT8FQ

Bu, Y., & Han, X. (2019). Promoting the development of backbone teachers through University-school collaborative research: The case of New Basic Education (NBE) reform in China. *Teachers and Teaching*, 25(2), 200–219. https://doi.org/10.1080/13540602.2019.1568977

Freire, P. (1972). *Pedagogy of the Oppressed*. London: Penguin.

Friesen, N. (2020). The technological imaginary in education, or: Myth and enlightenment in "personalized learning". In M. Stocchetti (Ed.) *The Digital Age and Its Discontents*. Helsinki: University of Helsinki Press. pp. 141–160.

Goel, A., & Camacho, I. (2020). Squirrel AI award for artificial intelligence for the benefit of humanity - An interview with Squirrel AI's Richard Tong. *Interactive AI Magazine*. 28 May. https://interactiveaimag.org/columns/articles/interview/squirrel-ai-award-for-artificial-intelligence-to-benefit-humanity/

Goldin, P.R. (2014). *Confucianism*. Abingdon: Routledge.

Hao, K. (2019). China has started a grand experiment in AI education. It could reshape how the world learns. MIT Technology Review. Accessed 16 September 2019. https://www.technologyreview.com/2019/08/02/131198/china-squirrel-hasstarted-a-grand-experiment-in-ai-education-it-could-reshape-how-the/

Ke, X. (2016). Person-making and citizen-making in Confucianism and their implications on contemporary moral education in China. In G. Zhao & Z. Deng (Eds.) *Re-envisioning Chinese Education: The meaning of person-making in a new age*. Abingdon: Routledge. pp. 116–129.

Kleinman, A., Yan, Y., Jun, J, Lee, S., Zhang, E., Tianshu, P., Fei, W., and Jinhua, G. (2011). *Deep China: the moral life of the person*. Berkley: The University of California Press.

Law, W-W. (2016). Cultivating Chinese citizen: China's search for modernisation and national rejuvenation. In G. Zhao & Z. Deng (Eds.) *Re-envisioning Chinese education: The meaning of person-making in a new age*. Abingdon: Routledge. pp. 34–54.

Lee, T.H.C. (2000). *Education in traditional China: A history*. Leiden: Brill.

Lin, C. (2013). *China and Global Capitalism: Reflections on Marxism, History, and Contemporary Politics*. New York: Palgrave MacMillan

Lin, D. (2017). *Civilising citizens in Post-Mao China: Understanding the rhetoric of Suzhi* (1st ed.). London: Routledge. https://doi.org/10.4324/9781315437170

Liu, Y-K. (2020). The Future of the Classroom? China's experience of AI in education. In *The AI powered state: China's approach to public sector innovation*. Nesta. pp.27–34 https://media.nesta.org.uk/documents/Nesta_TheAIPoweredState_2020.pdf

Liu, B., & He, Q. (2012). Personalisation and education in China. In Monica E. Mincu (Ed.) *Personalisation of education in contexts: Policy critique and theories of personal improvement*. Rotterdam: Sense Publishers. pp. 129–140.

Luckin, R., W. Holmes, M. Griffiths, and L. B. Forcier. (2016). *Intelligence Unleashed: An Argument for AI in Education*. London: Pearson Education. Available: http://oro.open.ac.uk/50104/1/Luckin%20et%20al.%20-%202016%20-%20Intelligence%20Unleashed.%20An%20argument%20for%20AI%20in%20Educ.pdf

Nemorin, S., Vlachidis, A., Ayerakwa, H.M., & Andriotis, P. (2022) AI hyped? A horizon scan of discourse on artificial intelligence in education (AIED) and development. *Learning, Media and Technology*. https://doi.org/10.1080/17439884.2022.2095568

Olson, P. (2018). Building brains: How Pearson plans to automate education with AI. *Forbes*. https://www.forbes.com/sites/parmyolson/2018/08/29/pearson-education-ai/#47c32cf41833

Pedersen, H. 2010. Is 'the posthuman' educable? On the convergence of educational philosophy, animal studies, and posthumanist theory. *Discourse: Studies in the Cultural Politics of Education*, 31(2). 237-250.

Rose, N. (1999). *Governing the Soul: The Shaping of the Private Self*. 2nd Edition. London: Free Association Books.

Siemens, G. 2013. Learning Analytics: The Emergence of a Discipline. *American Behavioral Scientist* 57 (10). 1380–400.

Tatlow, D.K. (2019). Manufacturing creativity and maintaining control. MERICS [Mercator Institute for China Studies] Report. 14 February. https://merics.org/sites/default/files/2020-04/190218_merics_ChinaMonitor_Creativity-in-education_A4_en_web_final.pdf

van Hooijdonk, R. (2019). The AI revolution is transforming schools and universities. *richardvanhooijdonk.com*. 11 October. https://blog.richardvanhooijdonk.com/en/the-ai-revolution-is-transforming-schools-and-universities/

von Radowitz, J. (2017). Intelligent machines will replace teachers within 10 years, leading public school headteacher predicts. *The Independent*. Available: https://www.independent.co.uk/news/education/education-news/intelligent-machines-replace-teachers-classroom-10-years-ai-robots-sir-anthony-sheldon-wellington-a7939931.html

Wells, K.J. (2020). Shifting gears: How Uber became an unchecked regulatory power in Washington, D.C. *Data and Society: Points*. 12 May. https://points.datasociety.net/shifting-gears-42ae36d31087

Yan (闫守轩), S., & Yang (杨运), Y. (2021). Education Informatization 2.0 in China: Motivation, framework, and vision. ECNU Review of Education, 4(2), 410–428. https://doi.org/10.1177/2096531120944929

Zhao, G. (2016a) China's historical encounter with the West and Modern Chinese education. In G. Zhao & Z. Deng (Eds.) *Re-envisioning Chinese education: The meaning of person-making in a new age*. Abingdon: Routledge. pp. 13–33.

Zhao, G. 2016b. Civilizational dialogue and a new understanding of the human person: implications for Chinese education as person-making, In G. Zhao and Z. Deng (Eds.) *Re-envisioning Chinese Education: the meaning of person-making in a new age*. Abingdon: Routledge, pp. 165–182.

Zhao, G., & Deng, Z. (2016). Introduction. In G. Zhao & Z. Deng (Eds.) *Re-envisioning Chinese education: The meaning of person-making in a new age*. Abingdon: Routledge. pp. 1–10.

8 Conclusions

This book has explored the relationships between artificial intelligence (AI) and education in China, principally through the juxtaposition of sociotechnical imaginaries of data-driven futures and analyses of social and political history. Through this approach, the chapters examined the role of policy and private sector entrepreneurialism, urban and rural dynamics, domestic and international flows of expertise, and 'personalising' platforms. All of these themes collaborate, intersect, and conflict in the production of China's AI-driven future, enunciated by government bodies, technology entrepreneurs, research institutes, policy analysts, and reporters, and constructed through urban zones of innovation, university qualifications, and data-driven software platforms. As such, this book, in its attempt to develop an overarching view of the relationships between AI and education in China, was only able to scratch the surface of a complex array of performative visions, all intent on reinventing a future of economic transformation and creative innovation, while at the same time constructing a present-day of data-driven efficiency and technocratic governance. Education appears thoroughly embroiled in this future-making, both as the engine of a vast conduit for the production of AI expertise and as the target of algorithmic interventions in the form of personalising platform software.

However, this book has also argued that such imaginaries are inflected by patterns, dynamics, and undercurrents from times past, which shape and mould the making of educational futures in China, and the coming-into-being of Chinese AI. Such a genealogical perspective surfaces 'histories of things that are supposed to have no history' (Ball 2013, p34). These include the broad refrains of humiliation, 'overcoming backwardness', and rejuvenation, all appearing to fuel an economic drive and entrepreneurial fervour delicately balanced on the shifting grounds of national identity and socialist ambition. As such, AI and education appear to have coalesced at the pressure points of exam competition, fused along the fault lines of regional inequality, and united for the cause of 'talent' generation. Excavating political and social history in China, as this book has only narrowly demonstrated, illuminates some of these trajectories in the relationships between AI and education, and sketches a terrain into which future projections can

DOI: 10.4324/9781003375135-8

be rooted. The following section summarises these key insights from across the previous chapters.

Visions and roots

Chapter 2 initiated a central orientation in this book, which was to attest to the power and perseverance of the government in China, in terms of the desire to control the coming-into-being of AI. In this sense, the vision of AI as a manageable and practicable technology, able to be exploited by the state for varying purposes and agendas, might be understood as particularly important in the context of China, where the form of government is highly centralised, at least in the ideological sense. The policy analysis in this chapter demonstrated the overt ambitions for state control, seemingly orientated principally towards economic transformation. As suggested, this policy functions as a high-level endorsement of, and direct incentive for, regions within China to assume responsibility for local development (Roberts et al. 2021), and higher education institutions appear to be positioned as key actors in these regional networks. This is a crucial part of understanding governance in China, which is too often presumed to function in straightforwardly uniform and hierarchical ways. The historical analysis in this chapter, which introduced some of the key political refrains that also featured in other chapters, offered a way of connecting the desire for the state management of AI with a deep-seated drive to boost national development through education and technology. This is a history that often appears to be overlooked or erased in the narratives of AI-driven national development. In an important sense, such insights divert attention from the more simplistic accounts of geopolitical rivalry, and foreground China's engagement with AI on its own terms.

Following from the analysis of policy, Chapter 3 developed the other side of the political economy of AI and education by examining the private sector, and in particular the ways a powerful imaginary is being constructed around the idea of vibrant communities of AI developers and entrepreneurs. Notably, a significant part of that vision, at least from an outside perspective on China, is of an array of viable companies into which foreigners might invest. Envisioning AI education companies as highly profitable businesses, ascending the networks of international venture capitalist funders, has very real consequences for how such businesses operate, and to whom they feel accountable. Especially where AI appears to be shifting into state education, this creates a significant tension between the vision of a successful tech firm on the one hand and an education provider on the other, with an arguably entirely different sense of responsibility towards the development and life trajectories of young people in China. Historical perspectives in this chapter focused on the precarious origins of the private sector in China, and the resurgence of private education in the 1990s. Such insights surface important hidden histories of AI entrepreneurialism in China, which appear to have been erased in the accounts of intensive innovation and economic success. These perspectives suggest a striking trajectory for business people in China, in which commercial activity is often perched on shaky ground. However, they also convey an engrained, almost survivalist enthusiasm for developing markets, which seems to be retained in the contemporary AI-driven educational industry. As such, a core tension between educational ideals and business demands seems to hold the sector together.

In many ways, Chapter 4 serves as an extension of the tussle between the state and private sector examined across Chapters 2 and 3. Indeed, this chapter stands out from the others in that it is not explicitly structured around the juxtaposition of sociotechnical imaginary and political history, but the analysis, nevertheless, builds upon the previous two themes. Focused on the stringent 'double reduction' regulations, this chapter confirms the centrality of the state in China, and demonstrates the precarity of the private sector. This is perhaps an important contribution to the wider research of sociotechnical imaginaries, which have shifted in recent years to more acknowledgement of the private sector as driving visions of the future (Mager and Katzenbach 2021). As Jasanoff suggests:

> Multinational corporations increasingly act upon imagined understandings of how the world is and ought to be, playing upon the perceived hopes and fears of their customers and clients and thereby propagating notions of technological progress and benefit.
>
> (Jasanoff, 2015, p27)

While the corporate shaping of the future is undoubtedly a factor in constructing the social order in China, the state still appears to hold considerable sway by dictating the narrative through policy and defining the means through which the private sector is able to participate. Moreover, as Chapter 4 concluded, there are indications that the 'double reduction' policy, whether intentionally or not, served to pull prominent education companies closer to the government, from which their AI products seem to become embroiled in state, rather than commercial, visions of the future. In this way, the overarching theme from Chapters 2–4 suggests a trend, beginning with liberation, where the promise of AI technologies are embraced through a central mandate to encourage technology development to flourish, as well as endorsing a new educational curriculum to support new generations of experts, but ultimately moving towards containment, where regulation is introduced to rein in the growing power of private firms through standards and principles. This trajectory demonstrates, not only the power of the Chinese government to both unshackle and restrain private enterprise where the greater benefit is perceived, but also the mutable ground on which the relationships between AI and education are situated.

Chapter 5 began with the history of Zhongguancun (中关村) as the spiritual home of China's technology community, but also as the origin of an imaginary of creative entrepreneurialism and urban agglomeration, which is being transplanted across China in the form of 'zones' of specialist innovation, often focused on AI. Here, universities appear to be positioned as key nodes in local networks, not only imagined to supply start-up companies with 'talent', but also to boost commercial AI research through dedicated institutes. As an example of some of these elite relations, the Shanghai and Hangzhou region is home to Squirrel AI, as well as Fudan University and Shanghai Jiao Tong University, ranking fourth and sixth respectively in China (QS 2020a). Southwest of Shanghai, Hangzhou has developed as a particularly well-known city for the tech sector, being the home of one of the largest Chinese internet companies, Alibaba, as well as a burgeoning start-up culture. It is also the site of Zhejiang University, ranked fifth in China (QS 2020a). The region of Shenzhen, Guangzhou, and Hong Kong encompasses both Hong Kong's historical prosperity as a centre for international finance and the modern metropolis of Shenzhen, home to Tencent. The wider region is also the site of Sun Yat-sen University in Guangzhou, ranked 8th in China (QS 2020a), and the University of Hong Kong, ranking 22nd globally (QS 2020b).

The historical context in this chapter surfaced one of the fundamental dynamics animating Chinese politics and society: the divide, and often substantial inequality, between urban and rural regions. The perspectives here provide an important sense in which cities have been historically privileged in China's developmentalist agenda, but also an appreciation of the ways rural areas have been a continual target of policy intervention, and positioned as a state priority. Both the development of AI for education and the shaping of national curricula for technical training in AI skills have been animated by these underling tensions. Not only have high-profile AI systems been envisioned to accelerate learning in deprived rural areas, but new programmes of study and accompanying qualifications have been produced to channel talented students into urban 'pipelines' of expertise. There are multiple imaginaries at work here, portraying AI as the solution to under-resourced regions, as well as a future industry of abundance in new 'mega city regions'.

Chapter 6 widened the focus from China's regional dynamics to the international stage, through an examination of the imaginaries of 'AI talent'. In this vision, not only are Chinese students trained in AI skills across the spectrum of education, but experts are enticed back to China for the purposes of enhancing the national AI profile. Chapter 6 thus examined the wide range of educational curricula, textbooks, and resources that are being developed to train new generations of AI workers, but also the transpacific trajectories of graduates and postgraduates, who increasingly seem to be seen as potential human capital by China and the US. Bolstering this nationalistic framing of AI training, a burgeoning area of 'national AI capacity' research was also suggested to contribute to the imaginary of data-driven geopolitical rivalry. That AI training and measures of 'talent' appear in some examples of this research is perhaps an example of the performative function of this imaginary, as nation states look to develop AI-infused educational curricula in order to move up the international rankings. Importantly, the historical perspectives in this chapter revealed a long tradition of Chinese students travelling to the US for study, focusing on Boxer Indemnity Scholarship students in the early 20th century who were seeking practical knowledge and technology that might modernise a 'backward' China. The concern for comparing national capacity in AI therefore seems to overlook and conceal a history of deep ties and knowledge exchange between China and the US, and subsequently, the unparalleled contribution that Chinese nationals have made to the development of AI internationally.

Chapter 7 sought to draw the previous discussions together, and focus the examination of AI on its direct impact upon students. The key vision explored here was that of 'personalisation', which is routinely portrayed as a radically beneficial form of teaching by advocates of AI. Personalisation was shown to envisage a kind of 'superhuman' teaching, in which students are provided with one-to-one AI systems that are infinitely knowledgeable, and always available. However, a closer examination of the 'knowledge space' functioning within such personalising platforms reveals a domain of rigidity, and the control of behaviour. 'Personalisation' is thus contrasted with 'personal choice', as well as concepts of student agency and subjectivity (Biesta 2009, 2015). The political and social history outlined in this chapter offered a further juxtaposition, in which a richer sense of subjectivity is developed through three themes: the 'divided self', drawing on China's transition into the 20th century; the 'entrepreneurial self', incorporating the market reforms of the late 1970s; and finally the 'creative self', outlining more contemporary views of constructivist educational practice in China. These perspectives, it is suggested, offer a much more nuanced view of subjectivity, identity, and the Chinese 'self' than is often acknowledged by the imaginaries of personalising AI, which tend to assume a narrow view of student-consumers. As such, the history of the 'self' in China, while only briefly articulated in Chapter 7, might be seen as a hidden history of Chinese AI, that has been concealed through the wider imaginaries personalising platforms and efficient one-to-one tuition.

Future directions for research

Future directions for this research might include the examination of issues of privacy and ethics in the development of AI for education in China. In recent years, the ethical dimensions of AI have become a high-profile concern. A great variety of ethical principles, guidelines, and frameworks have emerged in the past few years,[1] published by governments – for example, the US *Report on the Future of Artificial Intelligence* (Holdren et al. 2016) and *The European Commission's High-Level Expert Group on Artificial Intelligence* (Pekka et al. 2018), industry – for example, the *Microsoft AI principles*

(Microsoft Corporation 2019) and *Artificial Intelligence at Google* (Google 2018), as well as academic groups – for example, *AI4People* (Floridi et al. 2018) and the *AI Now 2019 Report* (Crawford et al. 2019). Against this international (although predominantly US and European) context, China has emerged as a prominent player in the development of the ethics of AI, formally with the announcement of the *Governance Principles for the New Generation Artificial Intelligence* (NGCNGAI 2019), as well as the *Beijing AI Principles* (Beijing Academy of Artificial Intelligence 2019).[2] In addition, and specifically in relation to education, China was a co-host of the UNESCO *International Conference on Artificial Intelligence and Education*[3] in 2019, and subsequent publication of the *Beijing Consensus on Artificial Intelligence and Education* (UNESCO 2019).[4] This has been an important development in considering education-specific aspects of AI ethics, which have been much slower to emerge in this policy milieu – another recent and notable example being an interim report from the newly formed 'Institute for Ethical AI in Education' at the University of Buckingham in the UK (Seldon et al. 2020).

Against this policy backdrop, extended research could consider how a particularly 'Chinese' form of ethical AI is being envisioned, given that China is now a key cultural context for the consideration of AI ethics globally (Gal 2020), and how such ideas might inform the development of ethical approaches to AI-infused education. Relatedly, such research might consider how education is being imagined to contribute to the development, dissemination, and understanding of AI ethics in the Chinese context. Here, historical (e.g. He 2015) and cultural (e.g. Stafford 2013) examinations of ethics in China may be essential to developing an in-depth understanding of the contexts into which 'ethical' Chinese AI technologies will be imagined, developed, and deployed, including specific considerations of ethical issues in education (e.g. Ke 2016). As Gal (2019) suggests, any understanding of ethics must arise, not just from the technical features of the design, or indeed from predefined policy frameworks, but rather from examining how technologies are used 'on the ground', in everyday societal consumption. Such an empirical approach may be a useful accompaniment to the analysis of sociotechnical imaginaries, and a key way of gauging the extent to which visions of 'ethical' AI perform particular kinds of educational futures.

Notes

1 For an extensive list of principle, guidelines, and frameworks see Hagendorff (2020).
2 The complex policy landscape *within* China requires unpicking, where it includes, for example, principles published by Tencent; Megvii; Baidu; the Artificial Intelligence Industry Alliance (AIIA); the Shanghai Advisory Committee of Experts on Artificial Intelligence Industry Security; the Center for International Strategy and Security, Tsinghua University; the Youth Work Committee of Shanghai Computer Society; and the Research Center for Brain-Inspired Intelligence, Chinese Academy of Sciences.

3 Further details available here: https://en.unesco.org/themes/ict-education/ai-education-conference-2019
4 For further details on UNESCO's work with AI and education see https://en.unesco.org/themes/ict-education/action/ai-in-education

References

Ball, S. (2013). *Foucault, power and education*. Abingdon, Oxon: Routledge.

Beijing Academy of Artificial Intelligence. (2019). Beijing AI principles. Retrieved June 18, 2019. https://www.baai.ac.cn/blog/beijing-ai-principles

Biesta, G.J.J. (2009). Good education in an age of measurement: On the need to reconnect with the question of purpose in education. *Educational Assessment, Evaluation and Accountability*, 2(1), 33–46.

Biesta, G.J.J. (2015). What is education for? On good education, teacher judgement, and educational professionalism. *European Journal of Education*, 50(1), 75–87 DOI: 10.1111/ejed.12109

Crawford, K., Dobbe, R., Dryer, T., Fried, G., Green, G., Kaziunas, E., Kak, A., Mathur, V., McElroy, E., Sánchez, A.N., Raji, D., Rankin, J.L. Richardson, R., Schultz, J., West, S.M. and Whittaker, M. (2019). *AI now 2019 report*. New York: AI Now Institute https://ainowinstitute.org/AI_Now_2019_Report.html

Floridi, L. et al. (2018). AI4People—An ethical framework for a good AI society: Opportunities, risks, principles, and recommendations. *Minds and Machines. https://doi.org/10.1007/s11023-018-9482-5*

Gal, D. (2019). Tech triangles and AI ethics: Danit Gal on Chinese AI. *China EconTalk*. Available: https://supchina.com/podcast/tech-triangles-and-ai-ethics-danit-gal-on-chinese-ai/

Gal, D. (2020). China's approach to AI ethics. In *The AI powered state: China's approach to public sector innovation*. Nesta. pp. 53–62. https://media.nesta.org.uk/documents/Nesta_TheAIPoweredState_2020.pdf

Google. (2018). Artificial intelligence at Google: Our principles. Retrieved January 24, 2019. https://ai.google/principles/

He, H. (2015). *Social ethics in a changing China: Moral decay or ethical awakening?* Washington, DC: Brookings Institution Press.

Holdren, J.P., Bruce, A., Felten, E., Lyons, T., & Garris, M. (2016). *Preparing for the future of artificial intelligence*. Washington, DC: Springer. pp. 1–58.

Jasanoff, S. (2015). Future imperfect: Science, technology, and the imaginations of modernity. In S. Jasanoff and S-H. Kim (Eds.) *Dreamscapes of modernity: Sociotechnical imaginaries and the fabrication of power*. Chicago, IL: University of Chicago Press.

Ke, X. (2016). Person-making and citizen-making in Confucianism and their implications on contemporary moral education in China. In G. Zhao & Z. Deng (Eds.) *Re-envisioning Chinese Education: The meaning of person-making in a new age*. Abingdon: Routledge. pp. 116–129.

Mager, A., & Katzenbach, C. (2021). Future imaginaries in the making and governing of digital technology: Multiple, contested, commodified. *New Media & Society*, 23(2), 223–236. https://doi.org/10.1177/1461444820929321

Microsoft Corporation. (2019). Microsoft AI principles. Retrieved February 01, 2019. https://www.microsoft.com/en-us/ai/our-approach-to-ai

NGCNGAI [National Governance Committee for the New Generation Artificial Intelligence]. (2019). Governance principles for the new generation artificial intelligence--developing responsible artificial intelligence. *China Daily*. 17 June 2019. Available: http://www.chinadaily.com.cn/a/201906/17/WS5d07486ba3103db f14328ab7.html

Pekka, A.-P., Bauer, W., Bergmann, U., Bieliková, M., Bonefeld-Dahl, C., Bonnet, Y., Bouarfa, L. et al. (2018). *The European Commission's high-level expert group on artificial intelligence: Ethics guidelines for trustworthy AI. Working Document for stakeholders' consultation*. Brussels. pp. 1–37.

QS. (2020a). QS mainland China University rankings 2019. *QS top universities*. Available: https://www.topuniversities.com/university-rankings/rankings-by-location/ mainland-china/2019

QS. (2020b). The University of Hong Kong. *QS top universities*. Available: https:// www.topuniversities.com/universities/university-hong-kong#wurs

Roberts, H., Cowls, J., Morley, J., Taddeo, M., Wang, V., & Floridi, L. (2021). The Chinese approach to artificial intelligence: An analysis of policy, ethics, and regulation. *AI & Society*, 36, 59–77. https://doi.org/10.1007/s00146-020-00992-2

Seldon, A., Luckin, R., Lakhani, P., & Clement-Jones, T. (2020). Interim report towards a shared vision of ethical AI in education. Available: https://www. buckingham.ac.uk/wp-content/uploads/2020/02/The-Institute-for-Ethical-AI-in-Educations-Interim-Report-Towards-a-Shared-Vision-of-Ethical-AI-in-Education.pdf

Stafford, C. (2013). *Ordinary ethics in China*. London: Bloomsbury.

UNESCO. (2019). Beijing consensus on artificial intelligence and education. Available: https://unesdoc.unesco.org/ark:/48223/pf0000368303

Index

Printed in the United States
by Baker & Taylor Publisher Services